need to know?

Speak Italian

Collins

First published in 2005 by Collins
an imprint of
HarperCollins Publishers
Westerhill Road, Bishopbriggs
Glasgow G64 2QT

www.collins.co.uk

A catalogue record for this book is available from the British Library

Editor: Caroline Smart
Text: Federico Bonfanti, Daphne Day
Other contributors: Julie A Quincey, Diana Grandi, Harry Campbell
Series design: Mark Thomson
Front cover photograph: Aldo Acquadro
© Look GmbH

isbn 0 00 7193319

Typeset by Davidson Pre-Press Graphics Ltd, Glasgow
Printed and bound by Scotprint, Haddington

Contents

Reference Zone

Introduction

Are you one of those people who want to learn Italian, but have never quite managed? Perhaps, after numerous attempts, you still don't feel on top of the basics. *Collins Speak Italian* is for you! This course is ideal for those with some knowledge of Italian, but who would like to learn more, or be shown that they do indeed know more than they think.

We do this through a series of dialogues. You can listen to the dialogues on CD1 and then explore the conversations in more depth in the book. The dialogues provide a snapshot of Italian while the points highlighted in each unit reveal how the language works - sometimes in a logical way, but often not!

We pick out of each unit the most important vocabulary, and then add a number of extra words to learn, often on a slightly different theme. Then it's your chance to speak Italian in the short exercises at the end of each unit.

The second part of the book, which relates to CD2, gives you the nitty-gritty - all the practical stuff that goes into a language - numbers, time, nouns, verbs and so on. Each section is tracked so you can decide what to focus on and there are lots of examples showing how Italian works. *Collins Speak Italian* is a basic introduction to the language. If you're looking for a dictionary to accompany this course, we recommend *Collins Easy Learning Italian Dictionary*.

So that you don't have to rely on listening to the CDs to get the pronunciation right, the book features an easy-to-follow pronunciation system. This means the book and CDs can be used independently. For a full explanation of how to use this course, turn to the *How to use* section on p14.

We hope that this original approach to language learning is one that works for you, and gives you the confidence to go on and speak Italian. You may even enjoy it!

Points about English

Mary works in a small grocer's shop. She sells cheese, fruit and vegetables. She gets up very early because the shop opens at 8 o'clock. She lives in a house in the centre of Manchester.

verbs and pronouns

These are the words that tell you the action of the sentence: **works**, **sells**. In English you use words like I, she or they (pronouns), with the verb to show who is doing the action: I **go**, you **go**, he **goes**, we **go**, etc. When it's not specified who is performing the action, you sometimes find the word 'to' in front of it: to work, to sell, to be. This is known as the 'infinitive'; you could think of it as the starting point for an 'infinite' number of ways that the verb can go.

nouns and articles

Nouns are labels for anything you can give a name to: **market**, **cheese**, **house**. A noun doesn't have to be a solid thing; it can be something abstract like **morning**, or it can be the name of something specific like a person or place: **Mary**, **Manchester** (such nouns, spelt with a capital letter, are called 'proper' nouns). When there is more than one of something, the 'plural' form is used; in English, this most often involves adding an -s (**markets**) though some words have irregular plurals (**man/men**, **sheep/sheep**). In English the definitive article is **the** and the indefinate article is **a** or **some**.

adjectives

Adjectives are words that describe a thing or person, to give extra information about them: a **small** market, a **tall** girl, **young** Mary, the work is **enjoyable**, Manchester is **big**. In English the adjective generally goes in front of the noun, and it's the same whatever the word it describes: **pretty** girl, **pretty** girls, a **slim** girl, a **slim** boy.

adverbs

An adverb is a word that describes a verb or an adjective – how, when or where something is done: Mary gets up **early**, she drives **carefully** and works **quickly**. Often, though not always, English adverbs are made by adding -ly to an adjective: **careful/carefully**; **quick/quickly**. But many of the most common adverbs do not follow this pattern: **early**, **fast**, **well**. Examples of adverbs applying to adjectives are **rather early**, **incredibly pretty**, **very good**.

prepositions

Prepositions usually indicate a relationship such as position or time: **in** a small market, **near** the centre of Manchester, **at** 8 o'clock. Sometimes one language uses a preposition where it is not needed in the other, just as you can say either 'I wrote to my mother' or (in American English) 'I wrote my mother'.

Points about Italian

Mary lavora in un piccolo negozio di alimentari. Vende formaggi, frutta e verdura. Si alza molto presto perché il negozio apre alle otto. Abita in una casa nel centro di Manchester.

verbs

In Italian the infinitive is just one word, such as **lavorare** 'to work', and there are different endings according to who is 'doing' the action: **lavora**'he or she works', **lavoriamo** 'we work', **lavorano** 'they work' and so on, where English usually has just two present tense forms: 'work' and 'works'. Italian verbs divide into three main sorts, according to the infinitive ending: **-are** (**lavorare** 'to work'), **-ere** (**vendere**, 'to sell') or **-ire** (**finire**, 'to finish'). Some of the most common verbs are irregular, just as they are in English.

nouns

Italian nouns are either 'masculine' or 'feminine'. Generally speaking nouns ending in **-o** are masculine, and those sending in **-a** feminine, though many nouns end in **-e** and these can be either masculine or feminine. To make nouns plural, you change the masculine ending **-o** to **-i** and feminine **-a** to **-e**. To make nouns ending **-e** plural, change **-e** to **-i**.

articles

The 'articles' **il/la** 'the' and **un/una** 'a', tell you the gender of the noun: **il negozio** 'the shop' (masculine), **la frutta** 'the fruit' (feminine). In the plural **il** becomes **i** and **la** becomes **le**. These are the most straightforward forms. You can see the full range in the Reference Zone.

adverbs

In Italian some adverbs are made by adding **-mente** to the adjective in its feminine form: **attiva** 'active' **attivamente** 'actively'. But many very common adverbs do not follow this pattern: **bene** 'well', **presto** 'early', **sempre** 'always'.

pronouns

To avoid repeating 'Mary', we use a pronoun, 'she', in subsequent references. In Italian, the verb ending usually tells you who is doing the action, so the pronoun can be dropped: **vende** rather than **lei vende**.

adjectives

In Italian, adjectives 'agree' with the noun they are describing. If a word is masculine, the adjective stays in the basic form in which you find it in the dictionary, such as **un piccolo negozio**, but if not, the feminine or plural endings may be needed. Adjectives usually go after the noun in Italian except for very common ones such as **piccolo** 'small', **bella** 'beautiful'.

prepositions

These work much as in English – **in** 'in, on', **su** 'on', **a** 'at'. However, Italian prepositions can combine with the articles: **a** + **il** = **al**, **in** + **il** = **nel**, etc. These can seem confusing, but when you get to grips with the articles things become clearer.

Pronunciation guide

To make it as clear as possible how to pronounce the Italian in the book, we've supplied a phonetic transcription (re-spelling) of each phrase. It's only intended as a rough guide, since it's not possible to represent Italian sounds accurately using English spelling. We use hyphens to break up words into syllables to help show how the stress works, and to make the transcription as clear and unambiguous as possible. Don't try to pronounce the syllables separately though, just run them together naturally as you would when speaking your own language. Italian pronunciation isn't difficult, and unlike English has the advantage of being predictable and logical. Once you learn a few basic rules, it shouldn't be too long before you can read straight from the Italian without bothering with the transcription. Here's a brief guide to pronouncing Italian.

The **consonants** are similar to Engish, with the following exceptions:

The letter **j** (pronounced as in English) is only found in foreign words like **il jogging** 'jogging'.

In Italian (unlike French and Spanish), **qu** is pronounced *kw*: **qui** *kwee*.

The letter **h** is always silent in Italian, though it can affect the way **c** and **g** are pronounced (see below). Apart from that use it only appears in foreign words such as **l'hotel**.

The letter **s** is pronounced *s*, except when it's between two vowels, when it's pronounced *z*. The same happens in the combinations **sb**, **sd**, **sg** and **sv**: **sveglio** ***zvel***-*yo*. To get the *s* sound between two vowels instead of *z*, you use a double **ss**: **casa** ***ka***-*za* but **cassa** ***kas***-*sa*.

The letter **z** is pronounced either *ts* or *dz*: **ragazzo** *ra*-***gat***-*tso*, **mezzo** ***med***-*dzo*.

When **c** comes before **a**, **o** or **u**, it's pronounced hard like an English k: **casa** ***ka***-*za*, **ricco** ***reek***-*ko*. Before **e** or **i**, it's pronounced soft like English 'ch': **cibo** ***tchee***-*bo*, **dice** ***dee***-*tchay*. When its followed by **h**, the effect is to give the hard sound, so **chi** is *kee* and **che** is *kay* instead of *chee* and *chay*: **chiave** ***kya***-*vay*, **anche** ***an***-*kay*. So you never get **cha**, **cho** or **chu** in an Italian word, as the **h** would be unnecessary. Before all other consonants, **c** is hard: **classe** ***klas***-*say*.

Meanwhile **sc** works something like **c**, being pronounced *sh* before **e** or **i**, and *sk* before other vowels or a consonant: **pesce** ***pesh***-*ay*, **pescare** *pes*-***ka***-*ray*, **boschi** is ***bos***-*kee*.

The letter **g** behaves just like **c**, pronounced soft like English j before e and i, and hard elsewhere. The letter **h** often serves to keep a **g** 'hard' (pronounced *g*) that would otherwise become 'soft' and be pronounced *dj*. For example, the plural of the word **lago** ***la***-*go* 'lake' is **laghi** ***lag***-*ee* rather than '**lagi**' (which would have to be pronounced ***ladj***-*ee*).

The combination **gl** is pronounced something like 'ly' in million, but run together as one sound: **figlia** ***feel***-*ya*, **degli** ***del***-*yee* (remember the hyphen is just to make the transcription clearer, it doesn't mean you separate the sounds).

A comparable thing happens with **gn**, which is a run-together 'ny' a bit like 'canyon' (**gnocchi** ***nyok***-*kee*, **bagno** ***ban***-*yo*).

The letter **r** is always pronounced, and should be rolled or tapped in your best operatic manner!

When a consonant is written double (**ss**, **tt**, **ll**) it's also pronounced double, in other words longer than a single consonant: **posso** ***pos**-so*, **bella** ***bel**-la*, **progetto** *prodj-**et**-to*. This isn't difficult, if you think of the first consonant as ending a syllable and the second one as beginning the following syllable. The same thing can happen between words in English, just not within a single word: picture the difference between 'my singing' (single 's') and 'mice singing' (double 's').

Vowels

In most English accents, the vowels tend to start in one place and move to another. For example, 'oh' starts as 'o' and moves towards 'oo'. But individual Italian vowels are always pronounced as a single pure sound:

a as in 'apple' – not as in 'April'
e as in 'set' – not as in 'sepia'
i like *ee* in 'sheep' – not like 'i' in 'ship' or 'shine'
o as in 'orange' – not as in 'open'
u like *oo* in 'soon' – not like 'u' in 'hut' or 'stupid'

However, there is nothing to stop two vowels occurring right next to each other, each keeping their original pronunciation, in words like **Dio** ***dee**-o* 'God'.

Stress

In both English and Italian, words with more than one syllable have 'stress', meaning that one part of the word is pronounced more emphatically than the rest of the word; for example in English we say '**mor**ning' not 'mor**ning**'. Mostly the stress in Italian falls on the next-to-last syllable but not always. When there's an accent written above a vowel, it marks the position of the stress: **città** (*tcheet-**ta***), **caffè** (*kaf-**fay***), but this is only marked in final syllables. However we show all stressed syllables in the transcription using ***heavy type***, so you won't be caught out.

useful websites

- **background info and reasons to learn Italian**
  http://how-to-learn-any-language.com/e/languages/italian/index.html
- **BBC 'Italianissimo' (online phrasebook)**
  http://www.bbc.co.uk/languages/italian/issimo/
- **audio phrasebook, survival phrases for travellers, word of the day and wine pronunciation guide!**
  http://italian.about.com/library/fare/blfarehome.htm
- **guide to irreglar verbs**
  http://turtiainen.dna.fi/cgi-bin/it/irreg.pl
- **a word about Italian regional dialects**
  http://www.netaxs.com/~salvucci/ITALdial.html

Dialogue Zone

The dialogues provide a snapshot of Italian, while the points highlighted show how the language works. We pick out of each dialogue the most useful vocabulary and then add a number of extra words to learn, often on a slightly different theme. Then its your chance to speak Italian in the short exercise on the following track.

How to use *Speak Italian*

The book comes with two CDs. Purple CD1, the Dialogue Zone, contains the dialogues, vocabulary and practice. Blue CD2, the Reference Zone, contains the nuts and bolts: numbers, days, months, etc. It goes with the final section of the book.

Dialogue Zone

There are 16 dialogues. Each one begins with an even track number: 2 is 'At the tourist office', 4 is 'A chance encounter' and so on. The practice sessions following each conversation begin with an odd number: 3, 5, 7, etc.

Try listening to the dialogues first, without referring to the book, to see how much you understand.

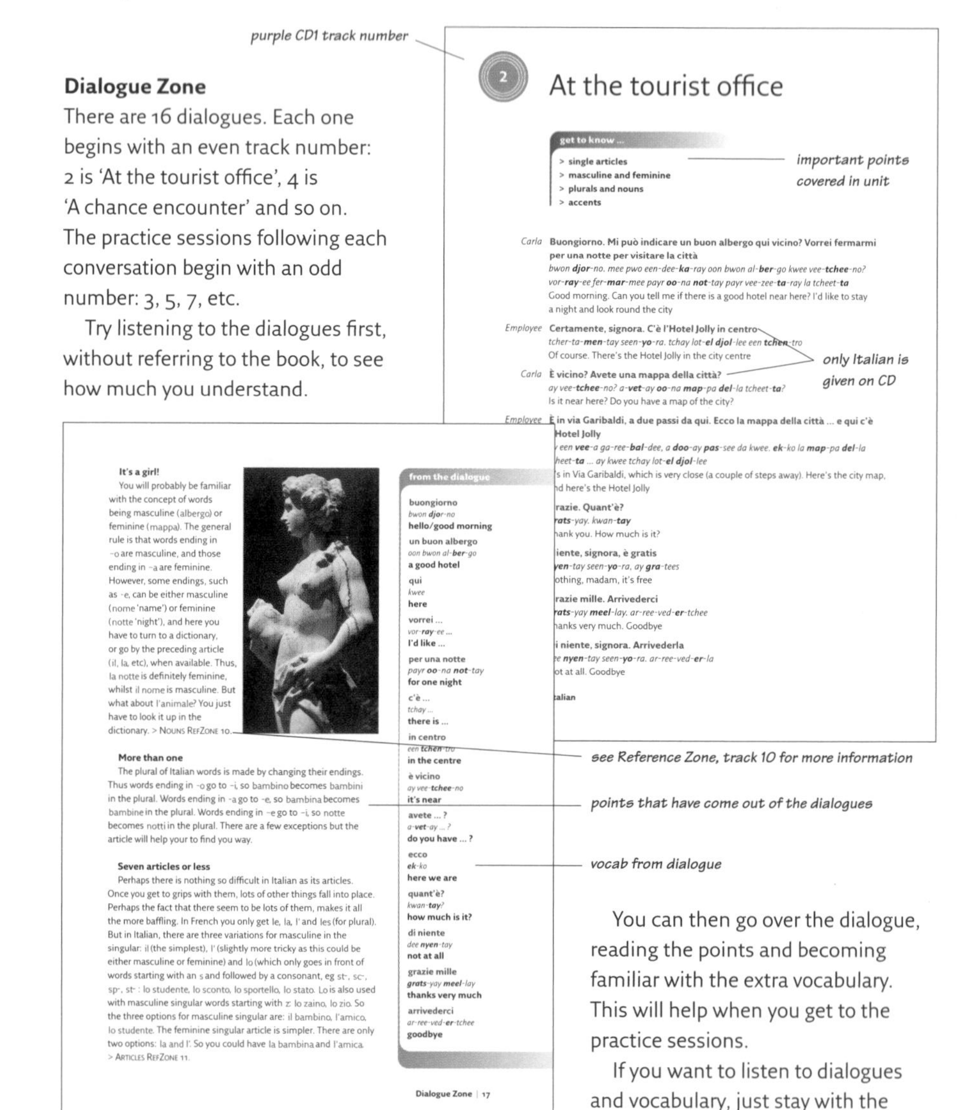

2 At the tourist office

get to know ...

> single articles
> masculine and feminine
> plurals and nouns
> accents

Carla **Buongiorno. Mi può indicare un buon albergo qui vicino? Vorrei fermarmi per una notte per visitare la città**
*bwon **djor**-no. mee pwo een-dee-**ka**-ray oon bwon al-**ber**-go kwee vee-**tchee**-no? vor-**ray**-ee fer-**mar**-mee payr **oo**-na **not**-tay payr vee-zee-**ta**-ray la tcheet-**ta***
Good morning. Can you tell me if there is a good hotel near here? I'd like to stay a night and look round the city

Employee **Certamente, signora. C'è l'Hotel Jolly in centro**
*tcher-ta-**men**-tay seen-**yo**-ra. tchay lot-**el djol**-lee een **tchen**-tro*
Of course. There's the Hotel Jolly in the city centre

Carla **È vicino? Avete una mappa della città?**
*ay vee-**tchee**-no? a-**vet**-ay **oo**-na **map**-pa **del**-la tcheet-**ta**?*
Is it near here? Do you have a map of the city?

Employee **È in via Garibaldi, a due passi da qui. Ecco la mappa della città ... e qui c'è Hotel Jolly**
*een **vee**-a ga-ree-**bal**-dee, a **doo**-ay **pas**-see da kwee. **ek**-ko la **map**-pa **del**-la heet-**ta** ... ay kwee tchay lot-**el djol**-lee*
s in Via Garibaldi, which is very close (a couple of steps away). Here's the city map, nd here's the Hotel Jolly

razie. Quant'è?
rats**-yay. kwan-**tay
hank you. How much is it?

iente, signora, è gratis
***yen**-tay seen-**yo**-ra, ay **gra**-tees*
othing, madam, it's free

razie mille. Arrivederci
***rats**-yay **meel**-lay. ar-ree-ved-**er**-tchee*
hanks very much. Goodbye

i niente, signora. Arrivederla
*e **nyen**-tay seen-**yo**-ra. ar-ree-ved-**er**-la*
ot at all. Goodbye

It's a girl!

You will probably be familiar with the concept of words being masculine (albergo) or feminine (mappa). The general rule is that words ending in -o are masculine, and those ending in -a are feminine. However, some endings, such as -e, can be either masculine (nome 'name') or feminine (notte 'night'), and here you have to turn to a dictionary, or go by the preceding article (il, la, etc), when available. Thus, la notte is definitely feminine, whilst il nome is masculine. But what about l'animale? You just have to look it up in the dictionary. > NOUNS REFZONE 10.

More than one

The plural of Italian words is made by changing their endings. Thus words ending in -o go to -i, so bambino becomes bambini in the plural. Words ending in -a go to -e, so bambina becomes bambine in the plural. Words ending in -e go to -i, so notte becomes notti in the plural. There are a few exceptions but the article will help your to find you way.

Seven articles or less

Perhaps there is nothing so difficult in Italian as its articles. Once you get to grips with them, lots of other things fall into place. Perhaps the fact that there seem to be lots of them, makes it all the more baffling. In French you only get le, la, l' and les (for plural). But in Italian, there are three variations for masculine in the singular: il (the simplest), l' (slightly more tricky as this could be either masculine or feminine) and lo (which only goes in front of words starting with an s and followed by a consonant, eg st-, sc-, sp-, st- : lo studente, lo sconto, lo sportello, lo stato. Lo is also used with masculine singular words starting with z: lo zaino, lo zio. So the three options for masculine singular are: il bambino, l'amico, lo studente. The feminine singular article is simpler. There are only two options: la and l'. So you could have la bambina and l'amica. > ARTICLES REFZONE 11.

from the dialogue

buongiorno *bwon **djor**-no* **hello/good morning**
un buon albergo *oon bwon al-**ber**-go* **a good hotel**
qui *kwee* **here**
vorrei ... *vor-**ray**-ee ...* **I'd like ...**
per una notte *payr **oo**-na **not**-tay* **for one night**
c'è ... *tchay ...* **there is ...**
in centro *een **tchen**-tro* **in the centre**
è vicino *ay vee-**tchee**-no* **it's near**
avete ... ? *a-**vet**-ay ... ?* **do you have ... ?**
ecco ***ek**-ko* **here we are**
quant'è? *kwan-**tay**?* **how much is it?**
di niente *dee **nyen**-tay* **not at all**
grazie mille ***grats**-yay **meel**-lay* **thanks very much**
arrivederci *ar-ree-ved-**er**-tchee* **goodbye**

Dialogue Zone | 17

You can then go over the dialogue, reading the points and becoming familiar with the extra vocabulary. This will help when you get to the practice sessions.

If you want to listen to dialogues and vocabulary, just stay with the even numbers.

Stressful accents

There are two types of accent in Italian: ` grave and ´ acute. Both show where the stress falls in a word when it doesn't follow the general rule ie on the second to last syllable. The grave accent is more common: citttà, lunedì, farò. It is also sometimes used to differentiate between words of one syllable which otherwise would look identical è 'is' and e 'and', là 'there' and la 'the', dà 'gives' and da 'from'. The only place you'll find an acute accent is on perché? (*payr-kay*), 'why?'.

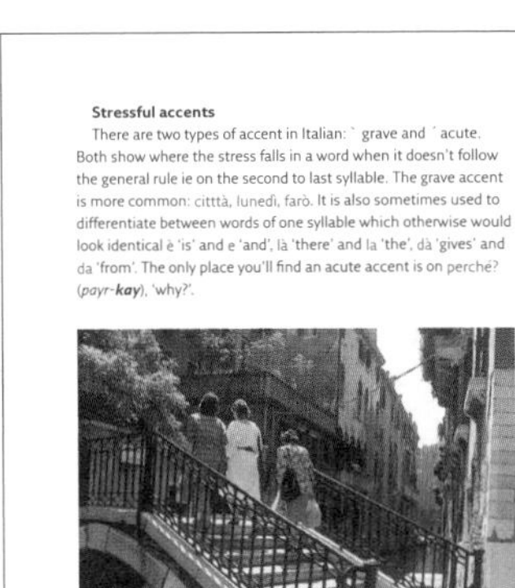

A near thing!

In idiomatic Italian, a due passi or a quattro passi da qui means literally 'two steps' or 'four steps from here'. These expressions are worth learning by heart because you're likely to hear them when people tall you the way somewhere, they'll make it much easier for you to get around.

Yes siree!

In Italian you don't have to use the words signore or signora all the time. Use them only when you encounter someone for the first time. The formality words is expressed by such as: vorrei ... 'I would like ...' or scusi 'excuse me' and does not require the use of signore or signora. To say goodbye formally, you have two options: arrivederci or arrivederla (the latter being rather more formal).

extra vocabulary

yes **no**
sì **no**
see *no*

ok
d'accordo/ok
*dak-**kord**-o/o-**kay***

perhaps
forse
***for**-say*

please
per favore/per piacere
*payr fa-**vor**-ay/payr pyatch-**er**-ay*

thanks
grazie
***grats**-yay*

hello *(day)/(evening)*
buongiorno/buonasera
*bwon-**djor**-no/bwon-a-**ser**-a*

hi/bye
ciao
tchao

goodbye
arrivederci
*a-ree-ved-**er**-tchee*

sorry
mi dispiace
*mee dees-**pyatch**-ay*

excuse me
scusi
***skoo**-zee*

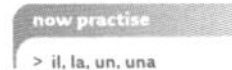

now practise 3

> il, la, un, una

Dialog

If you just want to test yourself, choose any odd-numbered track.

After each dialogue, you hear some useful vocabulary that has come out of it – first in Italian, then in English, and then in Italian again. Say the Italian the second time along with the CD to improve your pronunciation.

extra vocabulary

practice track number

8

Colours (red, blue, grey)

Colours agree with the noun they describe. Unlike in English, Italian colours follow the noun. So 'green ties' are cravatte verdi, not verdi cravatte.

black	nero(a) ***ner**-o(a)*	pink	rosa ***ro**-za*
blue	blu or azzurro(a) *bloo or ad-**zoor**-ro(a)*	purple	viola *vee-**o**-la*
brown	marrone *mar-**ro**-nay*	red	rosso(a) ***ros**-so(a)*
green	verde ***ver**-day*	white	bianco(a) ***byan**-ko(a)*
grey	grigio(a) ***gree**-djo(a)*	yellow	giallo(a) ***djal**-lo(a)*
orange	arancione *a-ran-**tcho**-nay*		

Rosa, viola and blu are 'invariable', which means they never change their endings, even in the plural. Generally speaking, blu is a darker blue and azzurro a lighter blue, but there is a generous overlap. 'Light' is chiaro and 'dark' is scuro. When these adjectives combine with a colour, to form a phrase such as 'light grey' or 'dark grey', then there is no agreement, so 'lots of dark grey cars' is molte macchine grigio scuro.

need to know

If someone has brown hair, the word castano(a), **meaning 'chestnut' is used** - dei capelli castani

what colour is it?	di che colore è? *dee kay ko-**lor**-ay ay?*
a blue door	una porta blu ***oo**-na **por**-ta blu*
the white sheet	il lenzuolo bianco *eel len-**swolo** **byan**-ko*
the yellow cups	le tazze gialle *lay tats-**say** **djal**-lay*
a light green shirt	una camicia verde chiaro ***oo**-na ka-**mee**-tcha **ver**-day **kyar**-o*

118 | Speak Italian

blue CD2 track number

extra tip

examples in use

Reference Zone

There are 33 tracks. You could think of it as a databank containing grammar, verb tables, numbers, days, months, times and so on. Each topic has a separate track. CD2 is useful for revision: it allows you to go back and choose what to practise, and it can also be used without referring to the book.

On the CD you hear a selection of the words and phrases shown in the book, as well as the most important tenses from the verb tables.

At the tourist office

get to know ...

- > single articles
- > masculine and feminine
- > plurals and nouns
- > accents

Carla **Buongiorno. Mi può indicare un buon albergo qui vicino? Vorrei fermarmi per una notte per visitare la città**
*bwon **djor**-no. mee pwo een-dee-**ka**-ray oon bwon al-**ber**-go kwee vee-**tchee**-no? vor-**ray**-ee fer-**mar**-mee payr **oo**-na **not**-tay payr vee-zee-**ta**-ray la tcheet-**ta***
Good morning. Can you tell me if there is a good hotel near here? I'd like to stay a night and look round the city

Employee **Certamente, signora. C'è l'Hotel Jolly in centro**
*tcher-ta-**men**-tay seen-**yo**-ra. tchay lot-**el djol**-lee een **tchen**-tro*
Of course. There's the Hotel Jolly in the city centre

Carla **È vicino? Avete una mappa della città?**
*ay vee-**tchee**-no? a-**vet**-ay **oo**-na **map**-pa **del**-la tcheet-**ta**?*
Is it near here? Do you have a map of the city?

Employee **È in via Garibaldi, a due passi da qui. Ecco la mappa della città ... e qui c'è l'Hotel Jolly**
*ay een **vee**-a ga-ree-**bal**-dee, a **doo**-ay **pas**-see da kwee. **ek**-ko la **map**-pa **del**-la tcheet-**ta** ... ay kwee tchay lot-**el djol**-lee*
It's in Via Garibaldi, which is very close (a couple of steps away). Here's the city map, and here's the Hotel Jolly

Carla **Grazie. Quant'è?**
grats**-yay. kwan-**tay
Thank you. How much is it?

Employee **Niente, signora, è gratis**
***nyen**-tay seen-**yo**-ra, ay **gra**-tees*
Nothing, madam, it's free

Carla **Grazie mille. Arrivederci**
***grats**-yay **meel**-lay. ar-ree-ved-**er**-tchee*
Thanks very much. Goodbye

Employee **Di niente, signora. Arrivederla**
*dee **nyen**-tay seen-**yo**-ra. ar-ree-ved-**er**-la*
Not at all. Goodbye

It's a girl!

You will probably be familiar with the concept of words being masculine (albergo) or feminine (mappa). The general rule is that words ending in -o are masculine, and those ending in -a are feminine. However, some endings, such as -e, can be either masculine (nome 'name') or feminine (notte 'night'), and here you have to turn to a dictionary, or go by the preceding article (il, la, etc), when available. Thus, la notte is definitely feminine, whilst il nome is masculine. But what about l'animale? You just have to look it up in the dictionary. > NOUNS REFZONE 10.

More than one

The plural of Italian words is made by changing their endings. Thus words ending in -o go to -i, so bambino becomes bambini in the plural. Words ending in -a go to -e, so bambina becomes bambine in the plural. Words ending in -e go to -i, so notte becomes notti in the plural. There are a few exceptions but the article will help you to find your way.

Seven articles or less

Perhaps there is nothing so difficult in Italian as its articles. Once you get to grips with them, lots of other things fall into place. Perhaps the fact that there seem to be lots of them, makes it all the more baffling. In French you only get le, la, l' and les (for plural). But in Italian, there are three variations for masculine in the singular: il (the simplest), l' (slightly more tricky as this could be either masculine or feminine) and lo (which only goes in front of words starting with an s and followed by a consonant, eg st-, sc-, sp-, st- : lo studente, lo sconto, lo sportello, lo stato. Lo is also used with masculine singular words starting with z: lo zaino, lo zio. So the three options for masculine singular are: il bambino, l'amico, lo studente. The feminine singular article is simpler. There are only two options: la and l'. So you could have la bambina and l'amica. > ARTICLES REFZONE 11.

from the dialogue

buongiorno
*bwon **djor**-no*
hello/good morning

un buon albergo
*oon bwon al-**ber**-go*
a good hotel

qui
kwee
here

vorrei ...
*vor-**ray**-ee ...*
I'd like ...

per una notte
*payr **oo**-na **not**-tay*
for one night

c'è ...
tchay ...
there is ...

in centro
*een **tchen**-tro*
in the centre

è vicino
*ay vee-**tchee**-no*
it's near

avete ... ?
*a-**vet**-ay ... ?*
do you have ... ?

ecco
***ek**-ko*
here we are

quant'è?
*kwan-**tay**?*
how much is it?

di niente
*dee **nyen**-tay*
not at all

grazie mille
***grats**-yay **meel**-lay*
thanks very much

arrivederci
*ar-ree-ved-**er**-tchee*
goodbye

What's so indefinite?

The indefinite article un tells you that the word which follows is masculine, eg un albergo. Uno also tells you that the following word is masculine, eg uno studente 'a student'- uno zio 'an uncle'. In una notte, the una shows that notte is feminine, even though the -e ending of notte doesn't let you know this by itself. And where a feminine noun starts with a vowel, the -a gets replaced with an apostrophe un'amica 'a lady friend', un'acqua minerale 'a mineral water'.

Macho English

Albergo means the same as hotel and both words are masculine. You should note that all English words used in Italian are considered masculine: il weekend, il computer, il whisky. Some English words, however, have their own particular meaning in Italian: il box 'a garage built next to your house', il footing 'jogging' and il lifting 'facelift'. Then there are some Italian words which look familiar, but mean something surprising: una camera, for example, is 'a bedroom', not something to take a picture with.

Greeting the day

The word buongiorno literally means 'good day' and it is used in Italy for a great part of the day, so it covers 'good morning' and 'good afternoon' (never 'buon pomeriggio'!) as well as 'hello'. After 5pm, Italians use buonasera, 'good evening'. The final greeting of the day is buona notte which is for when someone is actually going to bed, a bit like 'night night'. Buongiorno is the greeting you would use when entering the tourist office, a shop or a bar.

Accentuate the positive

When you see an accent two things happen. First you know where to put the 'stress' on the word – at the end. Second (and most important), you know that nouns ending in an accent don't have a plural form. So la città becomes le città and il caffè becomes i caffè.

Stressful accents

There are two types of accent in Italian: ` grave and ´ acute. Both show where the stress falls in a word when it doesn't follow the general rule ie on the second to last syllable. The grave accent is more common: citttà, lunedì, farò. It is also sometimes used to differentiate between words of one syllable which otherwise would look identical è 'is' and e 'and', là 'there' and la 'the', dà 'gives' and da 'from'. The only place you'll find an acute accent is on perché? (*payr-**kay***), 'why?'.

A near thing!

In idiomatic Italian, a due passi or a quattro passi da qui means literally 'two steps' or 'four steps from here'. These expressions are worth learning by heart because you're likely to hear them when people give you directions. They'll make it much easier for you to get around.

Yes siree!

In Italian you don't have to use the words signore or signora all the time. Use them only when you encounter someone for the first time. The formality is expressed by words such as: vorrei ... 'I would like ...' or scusi 'excuse me' and does not require the use of signore or signora. To say goodbye formally, you have two options: arrivederci or arrivederla (the latter being rather more formal).

now practise

> **il, la, un, un', una**

extra vocabulary

yes — **no**
sì — **no**
see — *no*

ok
d'accordo/ok
*dak-**kord**-o/o-**kay***

perhaps
forse
***for**-say*

please
per favore/per piacere
*payr fa-**vor**-ay/payr pyatch-**er**-ay*

thanks
grazie
***grats**-yay*

hello *(day)/(evening)*
buongiorno/buonasera
*bwon-**djor**-no/bwon-a-**ser**-a*

hi/bye
ciao
tchao

goodbye
arrivederci
*a-ree-ved-**er**-tchee*

sorry
mi dispiace
*mee dees-**pyatch**-ay*

excuse me
scusi
***skoo**-zee*

A chance encounter

get to know ...

- > **formal lei**
- > **adjectives**
- > **questions**
- > **agreement**

Sig.ra Ronconi **Buongiorno, signora Rossi. Come va?**
*bwon-**djor**-no, seen-**yo**-ra **ros**-see. **kom**-ay va?*
Good morning, signora Rossi. How are things?

Sig.ra Rossi **Bene grazie, e lei?**
***ben**-ay **grats**-yay, ay lay?*
Fine thanks, and you?

Sig.ra Ronconi **Bene, bene, grazie. E suo marito, come sta?**
***ben**-ay, **ben**-ay, **grats**-yay. ay **soo**-o ma-**reet**-o, **kom**-ay sta?*
Very well thanks. And your husband, how is he?

Sig.ra Rossi **Anche lui sta bene, grazie. Questo weekend pittura la cucina. E i suoi figli come vanno?**
***an**-kay **loo**-ee sta **ben**-ay, **grats**-yay. **kwest**-o week-**end** peet-**too**-ra la koo-**tchee**-na. ay ee **swo**-ee **feel**-yee **kom**-ay **van**-no?*
He's fine too, thanks. He's painting the kitchen this weekend. How are your children?

Sig.ra Ronconi **Oh, loro stanno benissimo. Adesso sono in vacanza, quindi può immaginare ...**
*oh, **lor**-o **stan**-no ben-**ees**-see-mo. a-**des**-so **so**-no een va-**kan**-tsa, **kween**-dee pwo eem-ma-djee-**na**-ray ...*
Oh, they are very well. They are on holiday now, so you can just imagine ...

Sig.ra Rossi **Bene, ora devo scappare, ma sono contenta d'averla incontrata. La saluto. Buona giornata!**
***ben**-ay, **or**-a **dev**-o skap-**pa**-ray, ma **so**-no kon-**ten**-ta da-**ver**-la een-kon-**tra**-ta. la sal-**oot**-o. **bwon**-a djor-**na**-ta!*
Well, I'll have to dash (escape) now, but I'm glad to have met you. I'll say goodbye. Have a nice day!

Sig.ra Ronconi **Grazie, altrettanto. Arrivederci!**
***grats**-yay, al-tret-**tant**-o. ar-ree-ved-**er**-tchee!*
Thanks, and the same to you. Goodbye!

Sig.ra Rossi **Arrivederci!**
*ar-ree-ved-**er**-tchee!*
Bye!

Call me Signora

In this dialogue we meet two ladies. Signora Ronconi addresses the other lady as signora Rossi, so this is quite formal. Her husband would be called signor Rossi (note how the final -e is dropped when signore is used with a name), but both he and his wife could also be addressed as signora Carla or signor Mario, using their first names. The word signorina exists for unmarried women, but it is becoming rather old-fashioned and women should all be addressed as signora, regardless of age or marital status. When signor and signora are used before someone's surname, like 'Mr' and 'Mrs' in English, they are abbreviated in writing to Sig. and Sig.ra. or Sra.

Why so formal?

The two ladies use the formal words lei and la. (These words are often written with capital letters.) This is the polite form which you use with older people, or people you don't know very well – or strangers such as people working in shops or restaurants. The verb ending for lei is the same one as for he and she, so lei is often used with the verb more to avoid any confusion. With your friends, as well as children, you use the familiar tu. In the plural there is no choice, it's voi for everyone – friends and strangers. The voi form can also be used instead of lei. In the tourist office Carla asked avete una mappa?, but she could have said ha una mappa? Both are correct.

Begging the question

When someone asks you a question and you want to ask them the same thing back, it's easy. You just say e lei? literally 'and you?' or e tu? if it's someone you use tu with. For example in the dialogue we have: come va? 'how are you?' And the reply, bene grazie, e lei? 'fine, thanks and you?' This also works where you make a statement about yourself and want to ask the same of them – spendo sempre troppo, e tu/lei? 'I always spend too much, do you?'

from the dialogue

come va?
***kom**-ay va?*
how are things?

bene grazie
***ben**-ay **grats**-yay*
fine thanks

suo marito
***soo**-o ma-**reet**-o*
your husband

come sta?
***kom**-ay sta?*
how is he?

sta bene
*sta **ben**-ay*
he's fine

i suoi figli
*ee **swo**-ee **feel**-yee*
your children

stanno bennissimo
***stan**-no ben-**ees**-see-mo*
they're very well

in vacanza
*een va-**kan**-tsa*
on holiday

devo scappare
***dev**-o skap-**pa**-ray*
I have to dash

buona giornata!
***bwon**-a djor-**na**-ta!*
have a nice day!

altrettanto!
*al-tret-**tant**-o!*
the same to you!/you too!

Do you agree?

Agreement is a key part of Italian. This means that the masculine form of an adjective is used with a masculine noun, and the feminine form for a feminine noun. And if the noun is in the plural, then a plural adjective is needed. The need for agreement means that signora Rossi says sono contenta, while her husband signor Rossi would say sono contento. > ADJECTIVES REFZONE 12.

Using a dictionary

When you look up an adjective in the dictionary, it is usually given in the masculine form, so you find contento for 'happy'. This shows that the adjective behaves in a regular way, it becomes contenta for feminine singular, contenti for masculine plural and contente for feminine plural. If you find verde 'green', you would be expected to know that this also follows a regular pattern: verde stays the same for both masculine and feminine singular, and that in the plural all -e ending words change to -i as in verdi. This applies to both adjectives and nouns, so animale verde becomes animali verdi in the plural (must be frogs!).

How goes it?

In Italian there are two ways of asking how things are. In this dialogue you have come va? literally 'how is it going?', and come sta? 'how are you?' or 'how is he/she?'. If you address someone as tu, the verb form is different: come stai?

Articles galore

Once you become familiar with the singular articles, then the plurals will fall into place. From being three singular articles for masculine words, you'll be relieved to find there are only two in the plural: i (for il) gli (for l' and lo). So il bambino becomes i bambini, l'amico becomes gli amici and lo studente becomes gli studenti. The feminine plural article is le (even for words beginning with vowels): le bambine and le amiche. > ARTICLES REFZONE 11.

Goodwill gestures

To reply to a polite phrase such as buona giornata 'have a nice day' you can use the phrase grazie, altrettanto 'thanks, you too'. You can also use it as a reply to buon appetito – 'enjoy your meal', provided that the other person is also eating.

The longest day

Did you notice in the dialogue that there were two different words for day? – giorno as in buongiorno and giornata as in buona giornata? There are a few other words where the added -ata can crop up, for example anno/annata – sera/serata – mattina/mattinata. The effect is to emphasize the actual duration of a span of time, and it's often used in set expressions to wish someone a good day, etc: buona serata 'have a good evening', buona mattinata 'have a good morning'. Buona annata is used to indicate that a certain year was a good one for wine, for example, 2003 was a good year for Chianti.

Questions made easy

Questions are simpler in Italian than in English. If you want to ask how signor Rossi is, you might just say sta bene?, 'is he ok?, with a questioning intonation, in other words, just raising slightly the pitch of your voice. Exactly the same words can be used to reply, without the questioning tone or the question mark, sta bene 'he's fine'. > QUESTIONS REFZONE 16.

Good stuff

Every language has conversational 'fillers', little words or expressions that are used not so much for their literal meaning as to fill a gap or move the conversation in a certain direction. Words like 'right', 'well', 'you know' are often used like this in English. Bene, says signora Rossi as she prepares to take her leave, 'right then' we might say in English, or 'anyway'. You'll need to understand them, and it's a good idea to learn to use them yourself as well. They help show that you are still speaking and reaching for the next thing you are going to say – very useful for learners! Here are some examples: allora 'so', 'then'; bene 'well' often abbreviated to beh!; mah 'well', 'let's see'; cioè 'that's to say'; insomma 'all in all'.

extra vocabulary

my family
la mia famiglia
*la **mee**-a fa-**meel**-ya*

my husband
mio marito
***mee**-o ma-**reet**-o*

my wife
mia moglie
***mee**-a **mol**-yay*

my children
i miei bambini
*ee **mee**-yay bam-**bee**-nee*

my son
mio figlio
***mee**-o **feel**-yo*

my daughter
mia figlia
***mee**-a **feel**-ya*

my parents
i miei genitori
*ee **mee**-yay djen-ee-**tor**-ee*

my father
mio padre
***mee**-o **pad**-ray*

my mother
mia madre
***mee**-a **mad**-ray*

my brother
mio fratello
***mee**-o frat-**el**-lo*

my sister
mia sorella
***mee**-a sor-**el**-la*

now practise

> **plural articles**

Meeting an old friend

get to know ...

> **informal tu**
> **negatives**
> **telling the time**
> **possessives**
> **prepositions**

Alfredo **Ma guarda chi c'è! Ciao Bruno, come va?**
*ma **gwar**-da kee tchay! tchao **broon**-o, **kom**-ay va?*
Well, look who's here! Hi Bruno, how are you?

Bruno **Bene grazie, e tu come stai?**
***ben**-ay **grats**-yay, ay too **kom**-ay **sta**-ee?*
Fine thanks, and how are you?

Alfredo **Non c'è male, grazie. Oggi non lavoro**
*non tchay **mal**-ay **grats**-yay. **odj**-ee non la-**vor**-o*
Not bad, thanks. I'm not working today

Bruno **Andiamo a bere qualcosa? Devo rientrare in ufficio tra un'ora**
*and-**ya**-mo a **ber**-ay kwal-**ko**-za? **dev**-o ree-en-**trar**-ay een oof-**fee**-tcho tra oon **o**-ra*
Shall we go and have something to drink? I have to be back in the office in an hour.

Alfredo **Perché no? Ho un appuntamento con mia madre alle sei, quindi ho tempo**
*per-**kay** no? o oon ap-poon-ta-**ment**-o kon **mee**-a **mad**-ray **al**-lay say-ee **kween**-dee o **tem**-po*
Why not? I'm meeting my mother at six, so I've got time

Bruno **Andiamo al bar in piazza?**
*and-**ya**-mo al bar een pee-**at**-tsa?*
Shall we go to the bar in the square?

(a little later)

Alfredo **Bene, grazie per la birra**
***ben**-ay, **grats**-yay payr la **beer**-ra*
Well, thanks for the beer

Bruno **Non c'è di che. Ciao e buona serata**
*non tchay dee kay. tchao ay **bwon**-a ser-**at**-a*
Don't mention it. Bye, and have a good evening

Among friends

You'll notice that Bruno and Alfredo don't use the polite, more formal, lei form with each other. They use the informal tu, partly because they are good friends, and also because they are younger and less formal than the two ladies in the previous dialogue. You can see this informality throughout the conversation in their choice of expressions such as ma guarda chi c'è 'look who's here' and ciao instead of buongiorno. Ciao is now used everywhere to mean both 'hi' and 'bye'. And e tu come stai? is an informal way of asking 'how are you?'

Oh my!

You might not think it, but 'your', 'my', 'his' are adjectives, known as possessive adjectives, because they show who possesses the noun. In Italian 'my', 'your', 'his', etc have to agree with what they are describing, not with the owner of the thing, as they do in English. So 'my mum' is mia madre, but 'my dad' is mio padre, while 'our son' is nostro figlio but 'our daughter' is nostra figlia. In Italian possessives are preceded by the article: il, la, l', etc, except in the examples we have just given, that is, when it refers to close family relations (oddly enough, in the singular only). Hence we have mia madre, mio padre and mio figlio, but la mia casa 'my house', il mio amico 'my friend' (masculine), le mie amiche 'my friends' (feminine plural). When talking about more than one relation – 'my brothers', 'my sisters', 'my children' – the article reappears: i miei fratelli, le mie sorelle, i miei bambini. > POSSESSIVES REFZONE 13.

from the dialogue

ciao
tchow
hi/bye

come stai?
kom-ay sta-ee?
how are you?

non c'è male
non tchay mal-ay
not bad

oggi
odj-ee
today

non lavoro
non la-vor-o
I'm not working

devo rientrare
dev-o ree-en-trar-ay
I have to be/get back

tra un'ora
tra oon o-ra
in an hour

perché no?
per-kay no?
why not?

alle sei
al-lay say-ee
at six

ho tempo
o tem-po
I have time

in piazza
een pee-at-tsa
in the square

non c'è di che
non tchay dee kay
don't mention it

buona serata
bwon-a ser-at-a
have a good evening

Counting the hours

In telling the time, the English expression 'o'clock' is not needed in Italian, but it is useful to know the words ora 'hour' and ore 'hours'. So, alle sei means 'at six o' clock'; literally 'at the six (hours)'. Italians regard time as a plural matter once it is past la una 'one o'clock'. 'What time is it? is che ore sono?, in other, rather clumsy words, 'what hours are they?' The answer to the question is sono le sei, or more simply, le sei '6 o'clock'. If you want to say that you are doing something 'in an hour', you need to use the preposition tra, eg devo rientrare in ufficio tra un'ora 'I must get back to the office in an hour'. > TIME REFZONE 4.

You're welcome

There are some words you wouldn't think to use since they don't have an equivalent in normal English speech. For example, when someone thanks you, you might reply: 'that's all right', 'you are welcome', 'my pleasure', 'no worries' or whatever. In Italian you have a number of useful expressions for 'don't mention it': non c'è di che as Bruno says or di niente which the man in the tourist office used. Prego is another such word.

Two for the price of one

The preposition a 'to', 'at', etc, often combines with the definite article il, la, lo, etc, to form one word. This is one of the things that learners have problems with. It all goes back to learning and understanding definite articles and how they change according to the gender, number and even how the noun begins (with a vowel or s + consonant). Once you have made sense of this, then the combining preposition makes sense. So a + il becomes al (andiamo al bar), a + la becomes alla (alla pizzeria) or, in the plural; alle sei 'at six' as we saw with the time. Other prepositions that combine with articles are di 'of', 'some', su 'on', da 'by', 'from', in 'in', 'into'.
> PREPOSITIONS REFZONE 15.

There is

C'è means 'there is' – an extremely useful phrase. We met it first at the tourist office where Carla asked if there was a hotel: 'c'è un albergo?'

Being negative

To make a negative statement in Italian you just put non in front of the verb. Non c'è male literally means 'there's nothing bad'. Alfredo says 'non lavoro' 'I'm not working'. > NEGATIVES REFZONE 17.

extra vocabulary

one uno ***oo**-no*	**eleven** undici ***oon**-dee-tchee*
two due ***doo**-ay*	**twelve** dodici ***dod**-ee-tchee*
three tre *tray*	**thirteen** tredici ***tred**-ee-tchee*
four quattro ***kwat**-tro*	**fourteen** quattordici *kwat-**tor**-dee-tchee*
five cinque ***tcheen**-kway*	**fifteen** quindici ***kween**-dee-tchee*
six sei ***say**-ee*	**sixteen** sedici ***sed**-ee-tchee*
seven sette ***set**-tay*	**seventeen** diciassette *dee-tchas-**set**-tay*
eight otto ***ot**-to*	**eighteen** diciotto *dee-**tchot**-to*
nine nove ***nov**-ay*	**nineteen** diciannove *dee-tchan-**nov**-ay*
ten dieci ***dyetch**-ee*	**twenty** venti ***ven**-tee*

now practise

> **negatives**

Asking the way

get to know ...

- > **directions**
- > **numbers**
- > **combining prepositions**

Diana **Scusi, signore. Sto cercando il museo d'Arte Moderna, ma mi sono persa**
__skoo__-zee seen-__yo__-ray. sto tcher-__kan__-do eel moo-__zay__-o __dar__-tay mod-__er__-na, ma mee __so__-no __payr__-sa
Excuse me, I'm looking for the Gallery of Modern Art, but I'm lost

Sig. Rossi **A, il museo d'Arte Moderna? È facile! Prenda la prima a sinistra, continui diritto fino al primo semaforo, poi giri a destra in via Garibaldi. Il museo è proprio di fronte**
a, eel moo-__zay__-o __dar__-tay mod-__er__-na? ay __fatch__-ee-lay! __pren__-da la __pree__-ma a seen-__ees__-tra, kon-__tee__-noo-ee dee-__reet__-to __fee__-no al __pree__-mo sem-__a__-for-o, pwoy __djee__-ree a __des__-tra een __vee__-a ga-ree-__bal__-dee. eel moo-__zay__-o ay __prop__-ree-o dee __fron__-tay
Ah, the Gallery of Modern Art? It's easy! Take the first on the left, keep straight on until you get to the first traffic lights, then turn right into Via Garibaldi. The art gallery is just opposite

Diana **Grazie, è lontano?**
__grats__-yay, ay lon-__ta__-no?
Thank you. Is it far?

Sig. Rossi **No, è a solo cinque minuti a piedi da qui**
no, ay a __so__-lo __tcheen__-kway mee-__noo__-tee a __pyed__-ee da kwee
No, it's only five minutes on foot from here

Diana **A, bene grazie. Senta, il museo delle Scienze, dov'è? Per caso si trova nella stessa zona?**
a, __ben__-ay __grats__-yay. __sen__-ta, eel moo-__zay__-o __del__-lay __shyen__-say, dov-__ay__? Payr __ka__-zo see __trov__-a __nel__-la __stes__-sa __dzon__-a?
Oh, that's great thanks. Oh, and where's the Science Museum? Is it by any chance in the same area?

Sig. Rossi **No, quello è dall'altra parte della città. Bisogna prendere l'autobus o andare in macchina**
no, __kwel__-lo ay dal-__lal__-tra __par__-tay __del__-la tcheet-__ta__. bee-__zon__-ya pren-__der__-ay __laoo__-to-boos o an-__da__-ray een __mak__-kee-na
No, that's on the other side of town. You need to take a bus or go by car

Diana	**Allora magari ci vado domani** *al-**lor**-a ma-**ga**-ree tchee **vad**-o dom-**a**-nee* Well then, maybe I'll go there tomorrow
Sig. Rossi	**Ci vada. È molto interessante** *tchee **va**-da. ay **mol**-to een-ter-es-**san**-tay* Yes, you should go – it's very interesting
Diana	**Grazie, signore e arrivederci** ***grats**-yay, seen-**yo**-ray eh ar-ree-ved-**er**-tchee* Thank you. Goodbye

Oy! You there

As we have already seen, the phrase mi scusi – or just scusi – is one way of getting someone's attention, just like the English 'excuse me!' You can also say senta (which literally means 'listen') both as a way to attract attention, or to signal that you are about to change topic, as happens in this dialogue when Diana asks about another museum to visit.

did you know ...?

Build up your Italian vocabulary quickly by noticing similarities with English. Continui is obviously like 'continue'. Giri 'turn' might sound very foreign, until you think of the English word 'gyrate'. Semaforo 'traffic lights' sounds very like semaphore, and if you think of it as giving signals, then this will help you recognise the word.

from the dialogue

scusi ...
***skoo**-zee ...*
excuse me ...

sto cercando ...
*sto tcher-**kan**-do ...*
I'm looking for ...

mi sono perso(a)
*mee **so**-no **payr**-so(a)*
I'm lost

è facile
*ay **fatch**-ee-lay*
it's easy

a sinistra
*a seen-**ees**-tra*
on the left

a destra
*a **des**-tra*
on the right

è lontano
*ay lon-**ta**-no*
it's far

a piedi
*a **pyed**-ee*
on foot

dov'è?
*dov-**eh**?*
where is it?

si trova ...
*see **trov**-a ...*
it's located ...

bisogna prendere
*bee-**zon**-ya pren-**der**-ay*
you need to take

ci vado
*tchee **vad**-o*
I'll go there

domani
*dom-**a**-nee*
tomorrow

The numbers game

Numbers come in two sorts. There are the ones you use for saying how many of something there are eg cinque minuti 'five minutes', sei ore 'six hours' and then there are the ones that help you put things in order: primo, secondo, terzo, 'first, second, third' etc. In the dialogue we see la prima a sinistra 'the first on the left'. So why has primo become prima? These numbers are adjectives and therefore have to agree with the noun they go with, in this case la strada 'road' which is feminine. Fino al primo semaforo, meaning 'as far as the first traffic light', has primo agreeing with masculine semaforo. Adjectives that have the masculine -o ending (like contento and primo) have a feminine -a ending (contenta and prima). Adjectives that end in -e, such as facile, difficile 'easy', 'difficult' have only that ending for masculine and feminine nouns. So you say il museo è interessante and la chiesa ('the church') è interessante. > NUMBERS REFZONE 3.

Are we there yet?

In spoken Italian you'll hear lots of ci meaning 'there', 'over there' etc, as in ci vado domani 'I'll go there tomorrow'. Ci vada 'do go there'. This ci is always used in Italian, whereas in English it may often be just implied – 'I'll go (there) tomorrow'.

The impersonal approach

A useful way of asking something is by using si plus the verb in the he/she form. Si trova ... ? 'is it located ... ?'; si può? 'can you?'; si mangia bene qui? 'do you eat well here?'. All simple short ways of finding out more.

Nella, della, dalla

These are the words that sometimes confuse people, the combining prepositions. Nella is perhaps one the least recognizable combinations; it's short for in la, as in nella stessa zona 'in the same area'. Della is 'of the' as in della città. And dall' is da + l' as in dall'altra parte. > PREPOSITIONS REFZONE 15.

did you know ...?

Key words to read signs

- > **destra** - **right**
- > **sinistra** - **left**
- > **uscita** - **exit**
- > **nord** - **north**
- > **sud** - **south**
- > **est** - **east**
- > **ovest** - **west**

Lost souls

Diana tells signor Rossi that she's lost (mi sono persa). Here we have the past tense of a reflexive verb, perdersi, 'to get lost'. Reflexive verbs take essere to make the past tense and the past participle (perso) agrees with the subject of the verb, so its a feminine ending persa. If it were signor Rossi, he'd say mi sono perso.

> VERBS REFZONE 20.

extra vocabulary

in the square
in piazza
*een pee-**at**-tsa*

at the market
al mercato
*al mer-**kat**-o*

in front of the station
davanti alla stazione
*da-**van**-tee **al**-la stats-**yo**-nay*

behind me
dietro di me
***dyet**-ro dee may*

at the cash desk
alla cassa
***al**-la **kas**-sa*

at the counter
allo sportello
***al**-lo spor-**tel**-lo*

near the beach
vicino alla spiaggia
*vee-**tchee**-no **al**-la **spyad**-dja*

in the village
nel paese
*nel pa-**yez**-ay*

after the traffic lights
dopo il semaforo
***dop**-o eel sem-**a**-for-o*

in the car park
nel parcheggio
*nel par-**ked**-djo*

in the newspaper
sul giornale
*sool djor-**na**-lay*

now practise

> **understanding directions**

10 At a café

get to know ...

> **object pronouns**
> **questions**
> **euros**
> **ecco**

Waiter **Che cosa desiderate?**
*kay **ko**-za dez-ee-der-**a**-tay?*
What would you like?

Silvia **Per me un cappuccino, grazie. E tu, Paolo, cosa prendi?**
*payr may oon kap-pootch-**tchee**-no, **grats**-yay. ay too, **paoo**-lo, **ko**-za **pren**-dee?*
A cappuccino for me, please. What will you have, Paolo?

Paolo **Una bottiglia d'acqua minerale. Ho sete**
***oo**-na bot-**teel**-ya **dak**-wa mee-ner-**a**-lay. o **set**-ay*
A bottle of mineral water. I'm thirsty

Waiter **Naturale o frizzante?**
*nat-oo-**ra**-lay o freets-**tsan**-tay?*
Still or sparkling?

Paolo **Frizzante, grazie. Con ghiaccio e limone**
*freets-**tsan**-tay, **grats**-yay. kon **gyatch**-o ay lee-**mo**-nay*
Sparkling please. With ice and lemon

Waiter **Ecco qua ... un cappuccino e un'acqua minerale. Volete un bicchiere in più per l'acqua?**
***ek**-ko kwa ... oon kap-pootch-**tchee**-no ay oon-ak-wa mee-ner-**a**-lay. vo-**let**-ay oon beek-**kyer**-ay een pyoo payr **lak**-wa?*
Here you are ... a cappuccino and a mineral water. Would you like an extra glass for the water?

Silvia **Sì, grazie. Avete del dolcificante?**
*see, **grats**-yay. a-**vet**-ay del dol-tchee-fee-**kan**-tay?*
Yes, please. Have you got any sweetener?

Waiter **Glielo porto subito**
***lyel**-o **por**-to **soo**-beet-o*
I'll get you some straight away

(returns with sweetener)

Waiter **È tutto?**
*ay **toot**-to?*
Is that everything?

Paolo **Sì. Quant'è?**
*see, **kwan**-tay?*
Yes, how much is it?

Waiter **Dieci euro**
***dyet**-chee **ay**-oo-ro*
Ten euros

Silvia **Offro io, Paolo. Ecco dieci euro**
***of**-fro **ee**-o, **paoo**-lo. **ek**-ko **dyet**-chee **ay**-oo-ro*
I'll get this, Paolo. Here you are, ten euros

Waiter **Grazie**
***grats**-yay*
Thank you

Silvia **Prego**
***preg**-o*
Not at all

Always asking

In this dialogue we see how easy it is to ask questions in Italian. When asking a yes/no question, all that is necessary is to give a rising intonation to a statement when speaking, or to add a question mark when writing: avete del dolcificante? 'do you have any sweetener?' or volete un bicchiere in più? 'do you want an extra glass?' There is no equivalent in Italian of the English question form 'do you...?' To ask 'what?' use che cosa, or more simply and less formal, cosa, with the verb: che cosa desiderate? 'what would you like?', cosa prendi? 'what are you having?' cosa vuoi fare? 'what do you want to do?' > QUESTIONS REFZONE 16.

from the dialogue

per me
payr may
for me

cosa prendi?
***ko**-za **pren**-dee?*
what will you have?

acqua minerale
***ak**-wa mee-ner-**a**-lay*
mineral water

naturale
*nat-oo-**ra**-lay*
still

frizzante
*freets-**tsan**-tay*
sparkling

con giacchio
*kon **gyatch**-o*
with ice

un bicchiere in più
*oon beek-**kyer**-ay een pyoo*
an extra glass

subito
***soo**-beet-o*
straightaway

è tutto?
*ay **toot**-to?*
is that everything?

quant'è?
*kwan-**tay**?*
how much is it?

prego
***preg**-o*
not at all

Long gone lire

Italy is in the eurozone. The word euro is masculine and invariable, so there is no plural in Italian: you can have un euro 'one euro' or dieci euro 'ten euros'. The euro breaks down into 100 euro cents, known as centesimi in Italian. As with pounds and pence, a price such as €1.50 is un euro e cinquanta – you state the number of centesimi (cents) without using the word.

Caffè, cappuccino, caffellatte ...

The standard type of coffee in Italy (un caffè) is an espresso: small (we're talking thimbleful), strong and black. If you prefer to have more coffee, but less strong, ask for un caffe lungo. If you want an equivalent to a filter coffee, ask for un caffè americano. If you want milk with your coffee you say con latte, or you can have un macchiato which is essentially a glass of milk with a dash of coffee. And although you find 'latte' outside Italy, caffellatte is normally what Italians have at breakfast. Of course, you can order un cappuccino, which may be slightly smaller than the servings you are used to. It is normally drunk by Italians as an 'elevenses', so don't be surprised by the look on the face of the waiter when you ask for a cappuccino after a meal!

did you know ...?

In a traditional bar/café, particularly at airports, where you drink standing up, you pay at the cassa (cash desk) and then go to the bar and ask for what you have paid for. It's also common to leave a little tip with lo scontrino 'chit' or 'receipt'. But if you sit inside or outside a café/bar, then you get a bill and pay when you leave (except in very busy bars). A useful phrase for asking 'how much is that?' is quant'è? literally 'how much is it?'

Un-pronouns-able words

You might be wondering what kind of word glielo is and how on earth you pronounce it. You probably won't even find it in the dictionary. It is in fact two pronouns stuck together: gli 'to (formal) you' and lo 'it'. It gets an e to glue them together. So glielo porto which means literally 'to you (gli) it (lo) I'll bring (porto)'. The 'it' or lo is referring to il dolcificante (masculine). If the waiter were talking about a receipt, la ricevuta, then he would say gliela porto where the la refers to the receipt or 'it' in English. And whereas 'it' has no gender in English, in Italian it must reflect the gender of the noun it replaces, so lo for masculine nouns and la for feminine nouns. When 'them' replaces a plural noun, this too must be masculine or feminine pronouns in Italian. > PRONOUNS REFZONE 19.

Ecco!

This is a very common word and you can make your Italian sound very natural if you use it often and with enthusiasm. It is used when giving someone something to mean 'here you are'. If you want to say 'here it is', you must, as usual bear in mind what 'it' is – if giving someone a glass (un bicchiere) or a cappuccino you would say eccolo! ***ek**-ko-lo!* – lo being used for the masculine thing. If it was a beer (una birra) or a cup (una tazza) you would say eccola. And if there were more than one glass or beer, you would use the plural, so eccoli (for glasses) and eccole (for cups). The same two words can be used when you see a friend arriving – if it is Marco you say eccolo! 'here he is!' and if it is Giulia you say eccola! 'here she is!'. When you arrive yourself, you can announce your arrival by saying eccomi 'here I am'.

now practise

> **numbers**

extra vocabulary

a glass of red wine
un bicchiere di vino rosso
*oon beek-**yer**-ay dee **veen**-o **ros**-so*

a cup of tea
una tazza di tè
***oo**-na **tat**-tsa dee tay*

red wine
vino rosso
***veen**-o **ros**-so*

white wine
vino bianco
***veen**-o **byan**-ko*

house wine
vino della casa
***veen**-o **del**-la **ka**-za*

a carafe of red wine
una caraffa di vino rosso
***oo**-na kar-**af**-fa dee **veen**-o **ros**-so*

a half of lager
una birra piccola
***oo**-na **beer**-ra **peek**-ko-la*

draught lager
una birra alla spina
***oo**-na **beer**-ra **al**-la **spee**-na*

still water
dell'acqua naturale
*del-**lak**-wa na-too-**ral**-ay*

sparkling water
dell'acqua frizzante
*del-**lak**-wa freet-**tsan**-tay*

Making friends

get to know ...

> **name and age**
> **reflexive verbs**
> **languages and nationalities**

Giulia **Ciao, io mi chiamo Giulia. E tu come ti chiami?**
*tchao, **ee**-o mee **kyam**-o **djool**-ya. ay too **kom**-ay tee **kyam**-ee?*
Hello, my name's Giulia. And you, what's your name?

Katy **Io mi chiamo Katy. Ho tredici anni. E tu quanti anni hai?**
***ee**-o mee **kyam**-o **kay**-tee. o **tred**-ee-tchee **an**-nee. ay too **kwan**-tee **an**-nee **a**-ee?*
I'm called Katy. I'm thirteen years old. And you, how old are you?

Giulia **Io ho quattordici anni. Di cognome mi chiamo Rossi. Tu abiti qui?**
***ee**-o o kwat-**tor**-dee-tchee **an**-nee. dee kon-**yo**-may mee **kyam**-o **ros**-see. too **ab**-ee-tee kwee?*
I'm fourteen. My surname is Rossi. Do you live here?

Katy **No, sono in vacanza con i miei. Abbiamo preso un appartamento in affitto vicino alla spiaggia**
*no, **so**-no een va-**kants**-a kon ee mee-**ay**. ab-**ya**-mo **pray**-zo oon ap-par-ta-**men**-to een af-**feet**-to veetch-**ee**-no **al**-la **spyad**-dja*
No, I'm on holiday with my parents. We're renting a flat near the beach

Giulia **Di dove sei?**
*dee **dov**-ay say?*
Where are you from?

Katy **Sono di Londra. Sono inglese. E tu, abiti qui?**
***so**-no dee **lon**-dra. **so**-no een-**glez**-ay. ay too, **ab**-ee-tee kwee?*
I'm from London. I'm English. What about you – do you live here?

Giulia **Sì, abito in centro e sono italiana. Studio inglese a scuola, ma non lo parlo molto bene**
*see, **a**-bee-to een **tchen**-tro e **so**-no ee-tal-**ya**-na. **stood**-yo een-**glez**-ay a **skwol**-a, ma non **par**-lo **mol**-to **ben**-ay*
Yes, I live in the city centre and I'm Italian. I learn English at school, but I don't speak it very well

Katy **Nemmeno io parlo bene l'Italiano!**
*nem-**men**-o **ee**-o **par**-lo **ben**-ay lee-tal-**ya**-no!*
Nor do I speak good Italian!

Age concerns

In English we 'are' a certain age, in other words we use the verb 'to be' to give the age of a person or thing. In Italian people 'have' a certain age, using the verb avere. Ho tredici anni 'I'm thirteen' Katy says when telling her age (how many years she has). She then asked Giulia e tu, quanti anni hai?, but she could have said e tu, quanti ne hai? (literally 'how many of them have you?'). She has just used the word anni, so it is clear that it is years that she is talking about. Ne is often used in this way: if Giulia told Katy she had lots of cats – ho molti gatti, she might well go on to ask Katy how many she has, quanti ne hai? 'how many have you got?'. In English you could say 'of them' but probably don't, but in Italian ne is necessary and Katy could go on to reply ne ho due 'I have two'.

To be or to have

As we've seen, Italian sometimes uses a different verb to English, for example avere 'to have' for people's ages rather than essere 'to be'. The same is true in French. The verb avere is also used when saying that you're hungry, thirsty, hot or cold: ho fame 'I'm hungry', ho sete 'I'm thirsty', ho caldo 'I'm hot'. If you are asking a friend whether they are hungry and so on, you ask: hai fame?, hai sete?, hai caldo?, hai freddo? It's the same for 'to be right' avere ragione or 'to be wrong' avere torto about something: hai ragione 'you're right', ho torto 'I'm wrong'. > Avere RefZone 26.

from the dialogue

mi chiamo ...
*mee **kyam**-o ...*
my name is ...

come ti chiami?
*kom-ay tee **kyam**-ee?*
what's your name?

ho tredici anni
*o **tred**-ee-tchee **an**-nee*
I'm 13 years old

quanti anni hai?
*kwan-tee **an**-nee **a**-ee?*
how old are you?

con i miei
*kon ee mee-**ay**-ee*
with my parents

in affitto
*een af-**feet**-to*
renting

di dove sei?
*dee **dov**-ay say?*
where are you from?

sono di Londra
***so**-no dee **lon**-dra*
I'm from London

sono inglese
***so**-no een-**glez**-ay*
I'm English

a scuola
*a **skwol**-a*
at school

nemmeno io
*nem-**men**-o **ee**-o*
nor do I

parlo bene l'italiano
***par**-lo **ben**-ay lee-tal-**ya**-no*
I speak good Italian

Lightning reflexes

Io mi chiamo Giulia – literally, 'I call myself Giulia' – is what's known as a 'reflexive verb'. They are more common in Italian than in English. For example, you can say in English 'I washed myself', but it sounds much more natural to say 'I washed'. In Italian you have to remember to add the bit that refers to whoever is receiving the action, even when there doesn't seem to be any action performed on oneself. 'I'm interested in cars' is: mi interesso di automobili literally 'I interest myself in cars'. Highly illogical, you may be thinking, but then, why should it be 'I enjoyed myself?' (mi sono divertito). Sometimes you just have to answer 'because that's the way it is' and not worry 'yourself' about it too much. > LAVARSI REFZONE 33.

Getting contractions

The Italian for 'near' is vicino a: vicino a Londra 'near London', vicino al museo 'near the museum', vicino alla spiaggia 'near the beach' and vicino ai negozi 'near the shops', vicino alle case 'near the houses', vicino agli sportelli 'near the windows'. These examples show how a combines with the articles il, la, i, le, gli to become al, alla, ai, alle, agli. This is how becoming familiar and confident with the articles and their behaviour, can help understand these combining prepositions. The word di (which can mean 'from' or 'of') behaves in the same way when followed by an article: il padre di Katy 'the father of Katy' or 'Katy's dad', but il padre del bambino, il padre della bambina. > PREPOSITIONS REFZONE 15.

Capital letters

In written Italian, countries have capital letters, as in English, but not nationalities (sono inglese 'I'm English', sono italiana 'I'm Italian'), or languages as in studio l'inglese 'I'm learning English'. The Italian for 'I' io is not written with a capital neither are the days or the months.

Surprising prepositions

Lots of things in Italian are guessable, but some prepositions may seem odd: sono in vacanza 'I'm on holiday', abito in centro 'I live in the town centre', vado in Italia 'I'm going to Italy', in affitto 'for rent'. All four phrases contain the familiar looking in – but only the second phrase is translated as you'd expect, so it is a good idea to learn whole phrases – a scuola, in vacanza, etc, rather than single words in isolation.

No place like home

It is essential to be able to say where you're from, where you're staying, where you're travelling to, and so on. In Italian a is used for a town as in a Londra, a Roma, a Pisa and in for a country or an area. So we have vado a Londra ma abito a Bristol 'I'm going to London but I live in Bristol' vado in Inghilterra ma abito in Italia 'I'm going to England but I live in Italy'. Note that if you say sono di Londra it means that you were born in London but could be living somewhere else: sono di Londra ma abito a Manchester 'I'm from London but I live in Manchester'.

Difficulties with -ese

As we have seen, words ending in -e can be either masculine or feminine. So sono inglese or francese or canadese 'I'm English' or 'French' or 'Canadian' can be said by either sex. The same applies to the noun (Englishman, Canadian etc) as to these adjectives - but surely the article (un/una) would be the giveaway? Well, yes and no. Before a vowel the una turns into un, so the only difference in writing between an Englishman (un inglese) and an Englishwoman (un' inglese) is that little apostrophe. And in speech they sound just the same.

extra vocabulary

I'm Irish
sono irlandese
*so-no eer-lan-**dez**-ay*

we're Scottish
siamo scozzesi
***sya**-mo skot-**tsez**-ee*

she is English
è inglese
*ay een-**glez**-ay*

he is Belgian
è belga
*ay **bel**-ga*

are you Italian?
è italiano(a)?
*ay ee-tal-**ya**-no(a)?*

they are American
sono americani
*so-no a-mer-ee-**ka**-nee*

she is American
è Americana
*ay a-mer-ee-**ka**-na*

he is Canadian
è canadese
*ay ka-na-**dez**-ay*

she is Australian
è australiana
*ay aoos-tral-**ya**-na*

now practise

> **asking questions**

Meeting family

get to know ...

> introductions
> fare
> da + present
> weather

Marco **Harry, ti presento mia nonna, che abita qui con noi**
__har__-ree, tee prez-__en__-to mee-__a__ __non__-na, kay a-__bee__-ta kwee kon __noy__-ee
Harry, this is my granny – she lives here with us

Harry **Piacere di conoscerla, signora**
pyatch-__er__-ay dee kon-__osh__-er-la, seen-__yo__-ra
Pleased to meet you

Sig.ra Bonfanti **Allora ti stai godendo le vacanze?**
al-__lor__-a tee __sta__-ee god-__end__-o lay vak-__an__-tsay?
So, are you enjoying your holiday?

Harry **Sì, grazie. Con questo bel tempo vado a nuotare tutti i giorni**
see, __grats__-yay. kon __kwest__-o bel __temp__-o __vad__-o a nwot-__a__-ray __toot__-tee ee __djor__-nee
Yes, thank you. With this good weather I go swimming every day

Sig.ra Bonfanti **Stai attento a non prendere un colpo di sole. Oggi fa molto caldo**
__sta__-ee at-__ten__-to a non __pren__-der-ay oon __kol__-po dee __so__-lay. __odj__-ee fa __mol__-to __kald__-o
Careful you don't get sunstroke. It's very hot today

Marco **Ma nonna! Non siamo più bambini**
ma __non__-na! non __syam__-o pyoo bam-__bee__-nee
Oh Granny! We're not kids any more

Harry **Sì, è vero. Fa molto caldo, ma mi metto sempre la crema solare e un cappellino**
see ay __ver__-o. fa __molt__-o __kald__-o, ma mee __met__-to __sem__-pray la __krem__-a sol-__a__-ray ay oon kap-pel-__leen__-o
Yes, you're right (it's true). It is very hot, but I always put sun cream on, and wear a hat

Sig.ra Bonfanti **Parli bene l'italiano, Harry. L'hai imparato a scuola?**
__par__-lee __ben__-ay leet-al-__ya__-no, __har__-ree. __la__-ee eem-pa-__rat__-o a __skwol__-a?
You speak good Italian, Harry. Did you learn it at school?

Harry **Sì, lo studio da tre anni**
see, __stood__-yo da tray __an__-nee
Yes, I've been learning it for three years

Marco **Beh, adesso andiamo in piscina. Ciao nonna! Ci vediamo più tardi**
*bay, a-**des**-so and-**ya**-mo een pee-**shee**-na. tchao **non**-na! tchee ved-**ya**-mo pyoo **tar**-dee*
Well, then, let's go to the swimming pool now. Bye granny! - see you later

Harry **Arrivederci, signora**
*ar-ree-ved-**er**-tchee, seen-**yo**-ra*
Goodbye signora

Sig.ra Bonfanti **Ciao, ragazzi. Divertitevi!**
*tchao ra-**gats**-tsee. dee-ver-**tee**-tay-vee!*
Bye bye boys. Enjoy yourselves!

Polite introductions

When you are introducing people to each other, remember to use the correct form. Because Marco is talking to his gran, he uses the familiar tu form and says, ti presento. This is the informal way of introducing people to each other. In a formal situation you should say le presento using the more formal lei form. Did you notice that Marco says mia nonna, rather than la mia nonna? This is because she is a close relation and you don't use the definite article with close relatives (but only in the singular), so you could have ti presento mio marito/mia moglie 'let me introduce my husband/my wife' or simply 'meet my ...'. If he were talking about his teacher, Marco would have said ti presento il mio professore.

from the dialogue

ti presento ...
*tee prez-**en**-to ...*
let me introduce ...

con noi
*kon **noy**-ee*
with us

piacere di conoscerla
*pyatch-**er**-ay dee kon-**osh**-er-la*
pleased to meet you

tutti i giorni
***toot**-tee ee **djor**-nee*
every day

stai attento!
***sta**-ee at-**ten**-to!*
be careful!

fa molto caldo
*fa **molt**-o **kald**-o*
it's very hot

è vero
*ay **ver**-o*
it's true

da tre anni
*da tray **an**-nee*
for the last three years

adesso
*a-**des**-so*
now

ci vediamo più tardi
*tchee ved-**ya**-mo pyoo **tar**-dee*
see you later

How long has this been going on?

When talking about how long you have been somewhere, or how long you have been doing something, you use da with the present tense of the verb: sono qui da una settimana 'I've been here for a week', la conosco da due anni 'I've known her for two years' and Harry's lo studio da tre anni, literally 'I'm learning it since three years', which translates as 'I've been learning it for three years'. If that literal translation sounds like something which an Italian speaker might say to you in their imperfect English, that's because they have trouble with this one too! When you want to ask 'how long...?' use the phrase da quanto tempo? (don't forget the da and present tense). So da quanto tempo stai qui? 'how long have you been here?', da quanto tempo la conosci? 'how long have you known her for?' and da quanto tempo studi l'italiano? 'how long have you been studying English? Note that we used the informal tu with these last three examples. > Time RefZone 5.

Fair weather

Whether it's good or bad, we all find ourselves talking about the weather. An important point to bear in mind is that while in English we say 'it is hot/cold etc', Italian uses the verb fare (usually translated as 'to do' or 'to make') fa caldo 'it's hot', fa freddo 'it's cold'. If you want to intensify the temperature, as in the dialogue, you add molto, so fa molto caldo 'it's very hot'. You might also want to say fa troppo caldo 'it's too hot'. And, remember, if you want to say that you yourself are too hot, you use the verb avere (not stare or essere) – ho troppo caldo 'I'm too hot'.
> Avere RefZone 26.

More for your fare

As well as weather, the verb fare is used in a number of expressions where you might not expect it. In English we say to 'pay' attention but in Italian it's fare attenzione. Other examples include fare la spesa 'to go shopping', fare una passeggiata 'to go for a walk', fare benzina 'to fill up with petrol' and finally fare la fila 'to queue up' (which is a rather alien concept to most Italians).
> Fare RefZone 28.

A little goes a long way

You can say a lot about the weather using only one verb form: piove? 'is it raining?', sì, piove 'yes, it's raining' or, hopefully, no, non piove 'no, it's not raining'. Or you might want to say piove da un'ora 'it's been raining for an hour', or be asked piove molto in Inghilterra? 'does it rain a lot in England?'. The answer could be sì, piove molto 'yes, it rains a lot' or no, non piove molto 'no, it doesn't rain much'. Unlike the different verb forms in English, the Italian verb remains the same, whether you are talking about what's happening at the moment, or what's happening in general, whether you are making positive or negative statements, or asking questions.

More 'wells' and 'buts'

Notice that, quite often, before making a statement, Italians tend to have little 'sighs'. This is a very idiomatic way of making a point. Hence ma! nonna simply means 'come on gran! And beh! is again another way of saying, 'come on, let's go'. You will hear a lot of these types of expressions.

extra vocabulary

it's raining
piove
***pyov**-ay*

it's snowing
nevica
***nev**-ee-ka*

it's windy
c'è vento
*tchay **vent**-o*

it's foggy
c'è nebbia
*tchay **neb**-bya*

it's hot
fa caldo
*fa **kald**-o*

it's cold
fa freddo
*fa **fred**-do*

what a lovely day!
che bella giornata!
*kay **bel**-la djor-**na**-ta!*

the weather is awful
il tempo è orribile
*eel **temp**-o ay or-**ree**-bee-lay*

a storm
un temporale
*oon tem-por-**a**-lay*

snow
la neve
*la **nev**-ay*

hail
la grandine
*la **gran**-dee-nay*

now practise

> **understanding weather forecast**

At a ristorante-pizzeria

get to know ...

> buono **and** bene
> commands
> using ne
> object pronouns

Dario **Buona sera. Un tavolo per due persone, per favore**
***bwon**-a **ser**-a. oon **tav**-o-lo payr **doo**-ay per-**so**-nay, payr fa-**vor**-ay*
Good evening. A table for two, please

Waiter **Accomodatevi. Ecco il menù e la carta dei vini**
*ak-kom-o-**dat**-ay-vee. **ek**-ko eel men-**oo** ay la **kar**-ta day-ee **vee**-nee*
Please sit down. Here's the menu and the wine list

(a little later)

Waiter **Avete scelto?**
*a-**vet**-ay **shelt**-o?*
Are you ready to order? (Have you chosen?)

Lucia **No, non ancora. Io sono vegetariana, che cosa mi consiglia?**
*no, non an-**kor**-a. **ee**-o **so**-no vedj-et-ar-**ya**-na, kay **ko**-za mee kon-**seel**-ya?*
No, not yet. I'm a vegetarian – what do you recommend?

Waiter **Dunque, come antipasto abbiamo la bruschetta. Come primo dei fusilli alle zucchine e basilico, e come secondo la pizza margherita**
***doon**-kway, **kom**-ay an-tee-**past**-o ab-**ya**-mo la broo-**sket**-ta. **kom**-ay **pree**-mo **day**-ee foo-**zeel**-lee **al**-lay tzook-**kee**-nay ay baz-**ee**-lee-ko ay **kom**-ay sek-**ond**-o la **peet**-tsa mar-ger-**ee**-ta*
Well then, we've got bruschetta as a starter. As a first course there's fusilli with courgettes and basil, and as a main course there's pizza margherita

Lucia **Grazie. Io prendo la bruschetta e i fusilli come primo, e solo un'insalata mista come secondo. E tu, caro, cosa prendi?**
***grats**-yay. **ee**-o **prend**-o la broo-**sket**-ta ay ee foo-**zeel**-lee **kom**-ay **pree**-mo, ay **so**-lo oon-een-sa-**la**-ta **kom**-ay sek-**ond**-o. ay too, **ka**-ro, **ko**-za **pren**-dee?*
Thank you. I'll have the bruschetta and the fusilli as a first course, and then just a mixed salad as my main course. What are you going to have, darling?

Dario **Io non sono vegetariano e la carne la mangio. Ma sono allergico ai gamberi. Negli spaghetti allo scoglio ce ne sono?**
***ee**-o non **so**-no vedj-et-ar-**ya**-no ay la **kar**-nay la **man**-djo. ma **so**-no al-**ler**-djee-ko **a**-ee **gam**-ber-ee. **nel**-yee spag-**et**-tee tchay nay **so**-no?*
I'm not vegetarian, and I eat meat. But I'm allergic to prawns. Are there any in the spaghetti?

Waiter **Sì, purtroppo ce ne sono. Le consiglio gli spaghetti alle vongole. Sono molto buoni**
*see, poor-**trop**-po tchay nay **so**-no. lay kon-**seel**-yo lyee spag-**et**-tee **al**-lay **von**-gol-ay. **so**-no **molt**-o **bwon**-nee*
Yes, unfortunately there are. I'd recommend the spaghetti with clams. It's excellent

Dario **Ok, li prendo. Allora, vorrei un antipasto misto poi spaghetti alle vongole e una bistecca come secondo**
*o-kay, lee **prend**-o. al-**lor**-a, vor-**ray**-ee oon an-tee-**past**-o **mees**-to pwoy spag-**et**-tee **al**-lay **von**-gol-ay ay **oo**-na bees-**tek**-ka **kom**-ay sek-**ond**-o*
Ok, I'll have that. So, I'd like mixed hors d'oeuvres, then the clam spaghetti, and a steak as my main course

Waiter **Desidera un contorno?**
*dez-**ee**-der-a oon kon-**tor**-no?*
Would you like any side dishes?

Dario **Delle patatine fritte, grazie**
***del**-lay pat-at-**ee**-nay **freet**-tay, **grats**-yay*
Some French fries, please

Waiter **Benissimo. E da bere?**
*ben-**ees**-see-mo. ay da **ber**-ay?*
Very good. And to drink?

Dario **Mezzo litro di vino rosso e una bottiglia di acqua minerale gassata, per favore**
***medz**-o **leet**-ro dee **vee**-no **ros**-so ay **oo**-na bot-**teel**-ya dee **ak**-wa mee-ner-**a**-lay gas-**za**-ta, payr fa-**vor**-ay*
Half a litre of red wine and a bottle of sparkling mineral water, please

(at the end of the meal)

Waiter **Avete finito?**
*a-**vet**-ay fee-**neet**-o?*
Have you finished?

Dario **Sì, grazie. Era tutto ottimo**
*see, **grats**-yay. **er**-a **toot**-to **ot**-tee-mo*
Yes, thank you. It was all excellent

Lucia **Ci porta il conto, per cortesia**
*tchee **por**-ta eel **kont**-o, payr kor-tez-**ee**-ya*
Could you bring the bill, please

from the dialogue

accomodatevi
*ak-kom-o-**dat**-ay-vee*
take a seat/sit down

avete scelto?
*a-**vet**-ay **shelt**-o?*
have you chosen?

non ancora
*non an-**kor**-a*
not yet

che cosa mi consiglia?
*kay **ko**-za mee kon-**seel**-ya?*
what do you recommend?

come antipasto
***kom**-ay an-tee-**past**-o*
for a starter

come primo
***kom**-ay **pree**-mo*
for a first course

come secondo
***kom**-ay sek-**ond**-o*
for a main course

sono vegetariano(a)
***so**-no vedj-et-ar-**ya**-no(a)*
I'm vegetarian

era tutto ottimo
***er**-a **toot**-to **ot**-tee-mo*
it was all wonderful

il conto, per cortesia
*eel **kont**-o, payr kor-tez-**ee**-ya*
the bill, please

Straight talking

Accomodatevi 'sit down, take a seat' is what the waiter says to his customers. Often in Italian it's possible to give a straightforward command (in the plural – to two or more persons) in a perfectly polite way, where we mealy-mouthed English-speakers might feel the need to add a 'please' or a question to soften the impact: 'would you like to sit down? Please take a seat! If you wouldn't mind signing here ... and so on.

> VERBS REFZONE 20.

Ghost words

To ask 'is there...?' or 'are there...?' you use c'è...? and ci sono...? So 'is there a lift?' is c'è un ascensore?, 'is there a problem?' c'è un problema? and ci sono gamberi negli spaghetti? 'are there prawns in the spaghetti?' The replies to these questions might be sì, c'è ne 'yes, there is'; no, non c'è ne 'no there isn't' and sì, ce ne sono 'yes, there are'. Did you notice the appearance of a word in Italian that seems to have no equivalent in the English? It's ne, which we met before in 'Making friends' with Katy and Giulia. And it exists in English only by implication to mean 'of it' or 'of them'. However, ne cannot be left out of Italian.

All well and good

It's easy to get confused between buono and bene. Buono is an adjective – something that describes a noun, so it's equivalent to 'good' as in 'a good pizza' una buona pizza and, in fact, is used very often to describe food: un buon formaggio 'a good cheese', un buon vino 'a good wine'. Buono is one of those adjectives that can go in front of the noun and it loses its final -o before masculine singular nouns, so una buona pizza but un buon vino. When it does follow the noun un vino buono, then the final -o reappears. Bene is an adverb, so it normally goes with a verb like the English 'well'. Note how bene is used in this dialogue: va molto bene 'that's absolutely fine' and va bene 'that's fine'.

Spaghettis and lasagnes

Lots of foods in Italian are plural, especially pasta: spaghetti, lasagne, fusilli. So when you talk about them, you use plural articles, adjectives and verbs. I fusilli and gli spaghetti are masculine, so the adjectives will be masculine plural: sono buoni gli spaghetti? 'is the spaghetti good?', le lasagne sono buonissime 'the lasagne is very good'. Did you notice the masculine plural article gli for spaghetti? This is because the word starts with sp-. It's one of the small things that often throws learners.

The object of your desire

When choosing what to eat, you may want to say 'I'll have it' or 'I'll have them'. Remember that the words for 'it' or 'them' will depend on what dish you are referring to: se c'è pollo arrosto, lo prendo 'if there's roast chicken, I'll have it' (lo because pollo is a masculine singular noun). Se c'è la bruschetta, la prendo 'if there's bruschetta, I'll have it (la because bruschetta is a feminine singular noun). Se ci sono degli spaghetti, li prendo (li because spaghetti is a masculine plural noun). Se ci sono delle lasagne, le prendo (le because lasagne is a feminine plural noun). Lo, la, li and le are object pronouns. > PRONOUNS REFZONE 19.

Come again?

This useful word translates in this dialogue as 'as'. The waiter says come antipasto, come primo, come secondo to indicate what is available by way of courses. You can use it too to say what you are having come primo, prendo ... 'as a first course, I'll have ...'. You can also ask what is available using the same word: cosa c'è come dolce? literally 'what is there by way of dessert?'

now practise

> **buono and bene**

extra vocabulary

to reserve a table
prenotare un tavolo
*pren-o-**ta**-ray oon **ta**-vol-o*

course/dish
il piatto
*eel **pyat**-to*

starter
l'antipasto
*lan-tee-**past**-o*

first course
primo
***pree**-mo*

main course
secondo
*sek-**on**-do*

dessert
dolce
***dol**-tchay*

fried
fritto(a)
***freet**-to(a)*

roasted
arrosto(a)
*ar-**rost**-o(a)*

grilled
alla griglia
***al**-la **greel**-ya*

baked
al forno
*al **forn**-o*

steamed
al vapore
*al va-**por**-ay*

Shopping

get to know ...

- > asking for things
- > da + person
- > quantities
- > types of ham

Bruno **Ehi, guarda. C'è un negozio di alimentari. Prendiamo due o tre cose per il picnic**
*ay-ee, **gwar**-da. tchay oon neg-**ots**-yo dee a-lee-men-**ta**-ree. prend-**ya**-mo **doo**-ay o tray **ko**-zay payr eel **peek**-neek*
Oh, look. There's a grocer's shop. Let's get a few things for the picnic

Sara **Va bene. Andiamo. Poi passiamo dal panettiere**
*va **ben**-ay. and-**ya**-mo. pwoy pass-**ya**-mo dal pan-et-**yer**-ay*
Ok then. Let's go. Then we can call in at the baker's

Shopkeeper **Buongiorno**
*bwon-**djor**-no*
Good morning

Bruno **Buongiorno. Vorremmo del prosciutto**
*bwon-**djor**-no. vor-**rem**-mo del pro-**shoot**-to*
Good morning. We'd like some ham

Shopkeeper **Crudo o cotto?**
***krood**-o o **kot**-to?*
Cured or cooked?

Bruno **Un etto e mezzo di prosciutto crudo, per favore**
*oon **et**-to ay **med**-zo dee pro-**shoot**-to **krood**-o, payr fa-**vor**-ay*
A hundred and fifty grams of cured ham, please

Shopkeeper **Ecco qua. Altro?**
***ek**-ko kwa. **al**-tro?*
There we are. Anything else?

Bruno **Un pacchetto grande di patatine**
*oon pak-**ket**-to **gran**-day dee pat-at-**ee**-nay*
A large packet of crisps

Shopkeeper **Sono sullo scaffale dietro di voi. Servitevi pure**
***so**-no **sool**-lo skaf-**fa**-lay **dyet**-ro dee voy. ser-**vee**-tay-vee **poo**-ray*
They're on the shelf behind you. Please help yourselves

Sara **Vorremmo del formaggio. Ha del gorgonzola?**
*vor-**rem**-mo del for-**madj**-o. a del gor-gon-**tzo**-la?*
We'd like some cheese. Do you have any gorgonzola?

Shopkeeper **Sì, certo. Quanto ne volete?**
*see, **tcher**-to. **kwan**-to nay vo-**let**-ay?*
Yes, of course. How much do you want?

Sara **Ma, faccia due etti, per favore**
*ma, **fatch**-tcha **doo**-ay **et**-tee, payr fa-**vor**-ay*
Oh, give me two hundred grams, please

Shopkeeper **Ecco fatto. Altro?**
***ek**-ko **fat**-to. **al**-tro?*
There we are. Anything else?

Bruno **Che cos'ha come frutta?**
*kay ko-**za** **kom**-ay **froot**-ta?*
What sort of fruit do you have?

Shopkeeper **Ho delle pere, mele, albicocche ...**
*oh **del**-lay **payr**-ay, **mel**-ay, al-bee-**kok**-kay ...*
I've got pears, apples, apricots ...

Bruno **Mi dia mezzo chilo di albicocche, grazie. Quanto le devo?**
*mee **dee**-a **med**-dzo **kee**-lo dee al-bee-**kok**-kay, **grats**-yay. **kwan**-to lay **dev**-o?*
Could you give me half a kilo of apricots, please. How much do I owe you?

Shopkeeper **Allora, in tutto sono nove euro e quarantacinque centesimi**
*al-**lo**-ra, een **toot**-to **so**-no **nov**-ay **ay**-oo-ro ay kwa-ran-ta-**tcheen**-kway tchen-**tez**-ee-mee*
Well then, that's nine euro and forty five cents in all

Bruno **Ecco a lei. La ringrazio**
***ek**-ko a lay. la reen-**grats**-yo*
Here you are. Thank you

Shopkeeper **Grazie a voi. Arrivederci**
***grats**-yay a voy. ar-ree-ved-**er**-tchee*
Thank *you*. Goodbye

from the dialogue

due o tre cose
***doo**-ay oh tray **ko**-zay*
two or three things

vorremmo del prosciutto
*vor-**rem**-mo del pro-**shoot**-to*
we'd like some ham

altro?
***al**-tro?*
anything else?

un pacchetto grande
*oon pak-**ket**-to **gran**-day*
a large packet

ha del gorgonzola?
*a del gor-gon-**tzo**-la?*
do you have any gorgonzola?

quanto ne volete?
***kwan**-to nay vo-**let**-ay?*
how much (of it) do you want?

mi dia ...
*mee **dee**-a ...*
could you give me ...

quanto le devo?
***kwan**-to lay **dev**-o?*
how much do I owe you?

in tutto
*een **toot**-to*
in total

la ringrazio
*la reen-**grats**-yo*
thank you

Tell me your deepest desires

We've noted the way a statement can be made into a question in Italian by raising the pitch of your voice slightly. It's most often a yes/no question that gets this treatent (avete finito? 'have you finished?', è tutto?, 'is that everything?) but you can find it elsewhere too, for example in this standard opener in shops, desiderate? 'what would you like?', it's as if you're leaving the other person to complete the sentence for you, 'you'd like ... what?'. The answer doesn't usually involve the verb desiderare 'to wish or desire', though, just say vorrei 'I would like' or as in this dialogue, vorremmo 'we would like'.

How much?

We've already come across the expression quant'è? in the cafè, now we hear quanto le devo 'how much do I owe you?'. You might be wondering what le is doing here. It isn't an article, it's a pronoun (of the indirect object kind!) meaning 'to you' (polite). If the informal was being used it would be quanto ti devo? > Pronouns RefZone 19.

Self-service

The verb servire crops up a lot in shop situations, and also at mealtimes. The Italians use it more often than we would say 'to serve'. In Italian it also means 'to need' or as in this very common phrase che cosa le serve? 'what do you need?' It is also used when telling someone to help themselves. The shopkeeper says servitevi pure 'go ahead, help yourselves'.

Weighing things up

Un etto, means a hundred grammes. This is how meat and cheese are weighed in shops, particularly 'delis'. But fruit and vegetables are sold by the kilo or half kilo. You can ask for mezzo chilo 'half a kilo' or un chilo 'a kilo'. Notice how an Italian kilo is written with ch-. This is because the letter k is used mainly for imported words and the sound 'k' is made in Italian using the ch letter combination.
On price labels, however, Kg is used as an abbreviation.

No 'small potatoes'

In Italian chips are patatine fritte 'French-fries'. But the same word patatine is used for crisps which come in a sacchetto 'packet'. Note that Italians are quite conservative in their tastes, so you won't find a wide range of flavours.

Many thanks!

You will often hear the phrase la ringrazio 'I thank you', as a slightly more polite variant of grazie. A shopkeeper or a waiter will sometimes reply, grazie a lei or a voi. If someone thanks you for something, you might respond with prego 'you're welcome'.

On the shelf?

In English we refer to the section where something is to be found; in Italian you usually specify the shelf lo scaffale followed directly by the name of the thing you want: lo scaffale della frutta/dei vini 'the fruit/wine section'. In a supermarket, you would use the word corsia to indicate the aisle something is in. So if you want to know where the sugar is, you might be told nella corsia dei dolci, 'in the bakery/cake aisle'. You'll also see this word corsia used on motorways where it means 'lane'.

did you know ...?

In Italy ham can be cooked (known in Italian as prosciutto cotto), or cured, that is, air-dried (known as prosciutto crudo, literally 'raw ham'). Parma ham is this type of ham. So if you ask for prosciutto, you will hear the shopkeeper asking crudo? or cotto?

Chez nous

Note in this dialogue that Sara says passiamo dal panettire 'let's go to the baker's'. In Italian this very idiomatic expression is used to describe popping in on someone: passo da mio cugino 'I'll pop in to see my cousin' or passo da Mario 'let's go round to Mario's'. Da can also be used with vado: vado dal dottore 'I'm going to the doctor's'. As usual, when da is used together with an article, you get the combined dal, dalla, etc. And da Mario can also mean 'at Mario's house'. If a friend phones you on your mobile asking dove sei? 'where are you?', you might reply sono da Mario. If you were out shopping, your reply might be sono dal panettiere 'I'm at the baker's.

now practise

> shopping

extra vocabulary

large
grande
***gran**-day*

medium
medio(a)
***med**-yo(a)*

small
piccolo(a)
***peek**-kol-o(a)*

a slice of ...
una fetta di ...
***oo**-na **fet**-ta dee ...*

a kilo of ...
un chilo di ...
*oon **kee**-lo dee ...*

200 grammes of ...
due etti di...
***doo**-ay **et**-tee dee ...*

a packet of ...
un pacchetto di ...
*oon pak-**ket**-to dee ...*

a tin of ...
un scattola di ...
***oo**-na **skat**-tol-a dee ...*

Buying shoes

get to know ...

- > **sizes**
- > **colours**
- > **piacere**
- > **comparative and superlative**

Assistant **Buongiorno, signora, posso aiutarla?**
*bwon-**djor**-no seen-**yo**-ra, **pos**-so a-yoo-**tar**-la?*
Good morning, madam, can I help you?

Lidia **Sì, grazie. Sto cercando un paio di scarpe blu con il tacco alto**
*see, **grats**-yay. sto tcher-**kand**-o oon pa-**yo** dee **skar**-pay bloo kon eel **tak**-ko **alt**-o*
Yes please. I'm looking for a pair of blue shoes with high heels

Assistant **Che numero porta?**
*kay **noo**-mer-o **por**-ta?*
What size do you take?

Lidia **Ho il trentanove**
*o eel tren-ta-**nov**-ay*
I take size thirty nine

Assistant **Un attimo. Vado a vedere se le abbiamo**
*oon **at**-tee-mo. **vad**-o a ved-**er**-ay say lay ab-**ya**-mo*
Just one moment. I'll go and see if we've got some

(comes back with a couple of pairs)

Assistant **Ecco qua, ho trovato questi due modelli**
***ek**-ko qwa, o tro-**vat**-o **kwes**-tee **doo**-ay mod-**el**-lee*
Here we are, I've found these two styles

Lidia **Posso provarli?**
***pos**-so pro-**var**-lee?*
Can I try them on?

Assistant **Certo! Prego, si accomodi**
***tcher**-to! **preg**-o, see ak-**kom**-od-ee*
Of course! Please take a seat

Lidia **Queste mi piacciono, ma mi vanno un po' strette. Non avete il numero più grande?**
***kwes**-tay mee **pyatch**-on-o, ma mee **van**-no oon po **stret**-tee. non a-**vet**-ay eel **noo**-mer-o pyoo **gran**-day?*
I like these, but they're a bit tight. You haven't got a bigger size, have you?

Assistant **Vado a vedere se c'è il quaranta. E l'altro paio non le piace proprio?**
__vad__-o a ved-__er__-ay say chay eel kwar-__an__-ta. ay __lal__-tro __pa__-yo non lay __pyatch__-ay __prop__-ree-o?
I'll go and see if we've got them in a forty. So you definitely don't like the other pair?

Lidia **No, il tacco è troppo alto**
no, eel __tak__-ko ay __trop__-po __alt__-o
No, the heels are too high

Assistant **Va bene, torno subito**
va __ben__-ay, __tor__-no __soo__-beet-o
Right, I'll be back at once

(shop assistant goes off to fetch a larger size)

Assistant **Mi dispiace, ma non abbiamo il quaranta in blu. L'abbiamo soltanto in marrone o in beige. Le vuole provare?**
mee dees-__pyatch__-ay, ma non ab-__ya__-mo eel kwar-__an__-ta een bloo. lab-__ya__-mo sol-__tant__-o een mar-__ron__-ay o een bezh. lay __vwol__-ay pro-__va__-ray?
I'm sorry, but we haven't got the forty in blue. We've only got it in brown or beige. Would you like to try them?

Lidia **No, grazie, mi servono proprio blu come il mio cappotto**
no, __grats__-yay, mee __ser__-vo-no __prop__-ree-o bloo __kom__-ay eel __mee__-o kap-__pot__-to
No thanks, I really need them in blue, to match my coat

did you know ...?

There are various words in Italian for 'size' in items of clothing. The basic word is la taglia, and this works for dresses, skirts, trousers and so on; for shirts, you traditionally specify the collar size, la misura del colletto, and with shoes, it's il numero as in che numero porta? 'what size do you take?' When answering, you can use the verb avere 'to have' or portare 'to take' as in ho il trentanove 'I take a 39'. Notice that Lidia says il trentanove because it is referring to il numero. If it were a dress, she would say porto la quaranta because it is referring to la taglia. Of course if buying clothes or shoes in Europe you'll need to know what you take in continental sizes!

from the dialogue

un paio di scarpe
oon pa-__yo__ dee __skar__-pay
a pair of shoes

che numero porta?
kay __noo__-mer-o __por__-ta?
what size do you take?

ho il trentanove
o eel tren-ta-__nov__-ay
I take a size 39

un attimo
oon __at__-tee-mo
just a moment

posso provare ...?
__pos__-so pro-__var__-lee ...?
can I try ...?

un po'
oon po
a little

più grande
pyoo __gran__-day
bigger

troppo alto
__trop__-po __alt__-o
too high

non le piace?
non lay __pyatch__-ay?
do you not like it?

torno subito
__tor__-no __soo__-beet-o
I'll be back at once

mi dispiace
mee dees-__pyatch__-ay
I'm sorry

Likes and dislikes

When Lidia tries on the shoes she says queste mi piacciono. The meaning is simple 'I like them', but grammatically her sentence might seem odd, since the subject is not 'I', but 'these', literally 'these are pleasing to me'. If you keep this in mind, you will understand why there are different verb forms in these two questions: ti piace Milano? 'do you like Milan?' and ti piacciono le scarpe? 'do you like the shoes?'. In English the verb is the same because the subject is 'you' in both questions. In Italian the verbs are different, singular piace in the first, and plural piacciono in the second. And the clue as to whether the verb should be piace or piacciono is in what is being liked. In the first it is Milan, so singular; in the second it is shoes, so plural.

Colours

When asking what colour something is, you say di che colore? – literally 'of what colour'. Colours used as adjectives follow the noun, 'blue shoes' is scarpe blu not blu scarpe. They also normally agree with the noun. So if Lidia had asked for some black shoes, she would have said delle scarpe nere (scarpe being feminine plural). But did you notice that blu didn't agree? This is one of the 'invariable' colours that doesn't change its ending at all. Other colours that are invariable are rosa 'pink' and viola 'purple' and beige. For light colours you use the word chiaro 'light' and for 'dark' scuro: so you'll have blu chiaro 'light blue' or blu scuro 'dark blue', verde chiaro 'light green', verde scuro 'dark green'.
> Colours RefZone 8.

I'm sorry, not displeased!

You should note that when the shop assistant says mi dispiace 'I'm sorry' (because she doesn't have the size 40 in blue), it has nothing to do with liking or disliking something or someone. It's used to express your feeling of 'sorrow' towards someone for something that occurred or that you cannot do for them. So if you find someone coming up to you for directions, and you have no idea what to say to them, you can say mi dispiace, non lo so 'sorry, I don't know'.

Comparatively comfortable

The shoes are a bit small and Lidia asks 'do you have a bigger size?' avete una misura piu' grande? This is a case where Italian is more straightforward than English, where some words take the -er ending (small - smaller) or use another word to make a comparison (**more** comfortable). In Italian the comparative is always made by adding più 'more', so 'bigger' is più grande, 'more interesting' is più interessante. When comparing two things, then you say più ... di, so Lidia e più giovane di Maria 'Lidia is younger than Maria'. To say that something is the biggest, tallest, etc (superlative), then the definite article is added: Lidia è **la** più giovane, 'Lidia is the youngest'; Paolo è **il** più ricco, 'Paul is the richest'.

Drop it!

In English you need to specify - 'do you like this/it/them' - but here's some good news: in Italian you can get away without that complication. People often use just piace? or piacciono when asking if you like something. If the assistant in a deli gives you a bit of cheese to taste, you might be asked piace? 'do you like it?, or a shop assistant might ask piacciono? 'do you like them?' instead of le piacciono queste cinture? 'do you like these belts?'.

now practise

> **colours**

extra vocabulary

a green skirt
una gonna verde
***oo**-na **gon**-na **ver**-day*

a pink t-shirt
una maglietta rosa
***oo**-na mal-**yet**-ta **ro**-za*

a red blouse
una camicetta rossa
***oo**-na ka-mee-**tchet**-ta **ros**-sa*

brown trousers
pantaloni marroni
*pan-ta-**lo**-nee mar-**ro**-nee*

black gloves
guanti neri
*__gwan__-tee **ner**-ee*

a white shirt
una camicia bianca
*__oo__-na ka-**meetch**-a **byan**-ka*

a grey jacket
una giacca grigia
*__oo__-na **djak**-ka **gree**-dja*

a pair of sandals
un paio di sandali
*oon **pa**-yo dee **san**-da-lee*

trainers
le scarpe di ginnastica
*lay **skar**-pay dee djeen-**nas**-tee-ka*

At the station

get to know ...

> c'è **and** ci sono
> **time**
> per + **destination**

Anna **Buongiorno, vorrei un biglietto per Venezia, per favore**
*bwon-**djor**-no, vor-**ray**-ee oon beel-**yet**-to payr ven-**ets**-ya, payr fa-**vor**-ay*
Good morning, I'd like a ticket to Venice, please

Assistant **Andata e ritorno?**
*an-**da**-ta ay ree-**tor**-no?*
Return?

Anna **No, solo andata. Scusi, a che ora arriva il treno a Venezia?**
*no, **so**-lo an-**da**-ta. **skoo**-zee, a kay **o**-ra ar-**ree**-va eel **tren**-o a ven-**ets**-ya?*
No, a single only. Please could you tell me what time the train arrives in Venice?

Assistant **Dunque, ci sono due treni. Il primo è un Eurostar che parte alle undici e otto e arriva a Venezia alle sedici e tre. Questo treno è diretto. Il secondo impiega di più e bisogna cambiare. È un Espresso e costa di meno**
***doon**-kway, tchee **so**-no **doo**-ay **tren**-ee. eel **pree**-mo ay oon **eoo**-ro-star kay **par**-tay **al**-lay **oon**-dee-tchee ay **ot**-to ay ar-**ree**-va a ven-**ets**-ya **al**-lay **sed**-ee-tchee ay tray. **kwest**-o **tren**-o ay dee-**ret**-to. eel sek-**on**-do eemp-**yeg**-a dee pyoo ay bee-**zon**-ya kamb-**ya**-ray. ay oon es-**pres**-so ay **kos**-ta dee **men**-o*
Let's see then, there are two trains. The first is a Eurostar which leaves at eight minutes past eleven and arrives in Venice at 16.03. It's a direct train. The second one takes longer and you have to change. It's a stopping train and it's cheaper

Anna **Va bene, prendo l'Eurostar. Quanto costa il biglietto?**
*va **ben**-ay, **prend**-o **leoo**-ro-star. **kwant**-o **kos**-ta eel beel-**yet**-to?*
Okay, I'll take the Eurostar. How much does the ticket cost?

Assistant **Sono settanta euro e sessanta in seconda classe, compresa la prenotazione, che è obbligatoria sull'Eurostar. Confermo?**
***so**-no set-**tan**-ta **ay**-oo-ro e ses-**san**-ta een sek-**on**-da **klas**-say, kom-**prez**-a la pray-no-tats-**yo**-nay, kay ay ob-blee-ga-**tor**-ya sool-**leoo**-ro-star. kon-**fer**-mo?*
It's seventy euros sixty for a second class ticket, including the booking charge, which is obligatory on Eurostar. Shall I go ahead?

Anna **Sì, va bene. Grazie**
*see, va **ben**-ay. **grats**-yay*
Yes, that's fine. Thank you

Assistant **Ha per caso diritto a qualche sconto?**
*a payr **ka**-zo dee-**reet**-to a **kwal**-kay **skont**-o*
Are you entitled to a reduction, by any chance?

Anna **Sì, ho la Carta d'Argento**
*see, o la **kar**-ta dar-**djen**-to*
Yes, I've got a Carta Argento (senior railcard)

Assistant **Allora ha diritto al trenta per cento di sconto. In totale sono ...**
*al-**lor**-a a dee-**reet**-to al **tren**-ta payr **tchen**-to dee **skont**-o. een tot-**al**-ay **so**-no ...*
So that means you're entitled to a thirty percent reduction. In total that's ...

(on the platform)

Anna **Scusi, da che binario parte l'Eurostar?**
***skoo**-zee, da kay bee-**nar**-yo **par**-tay **leoo**-ro-star?*
Excuse me, which platform does the Eurostar go from?

Porter **Dal binario numero due**
*dal bee-**nar**-yo **noo**-mer-o **doo**-ay*
From platform number two

Anna **Questo qui è il binario due?**
***kwest**-o kwee ay eel bee-**nar**-yo **doo**-ay?*
Is this one platform two?

Porter **No, questo è il tre. Quello là è il due**
*no **kwest**-o ay eel tray. **kwel**-lo la ay eel **doo**-ay*
No, this is platform three. That one over there is platform two

from the dialogue

un biglietto per Venezia
*oon beel-**yet**-to payr ven-**ets**-ya*
a ticket to Venice

andata e ritorno
*an-**da**-ta ay ree-**tor**-no*
return

solo andata
***so**-lo an-**da**-ta*
single only

a che ora?
*a kay **o**-ra?*
at what time?

ci sono ...
*tchee **so**-no ...*
there are ...

impiega di più
*eemp-**yeg**-a dee pyoo*
it takes longer

bisogna cambiare
*bee-**zon**-ya kamb-**ya**-ray*
you have to change

qualche sconto
***kwal**-kay **skont**-o*
some reduction

questo qui
***kwest**-o kwee*
this one here

quello là
***kwel**-lo la*
that one there

did you know ...?

The railways in Italy (unlike in Britain!) are relatively cheap and they provide, on the whole, a good national service. Basically, the more you pay, the faster you travel. The names of trains are an indication of how quickly they can get you to your destination – Eurostar – Inter City – Espresso and so on. Some trains carry a supplement – un supplemento – which you should pay before you get on board (or else it costs more), and on some of the fast trains it is compulsory to book a seat. Check out what is on offer at www.trenitalia.com.

Cheap as chips

The Italian translation for 'cheap' is a buon mercato. But this is really only used when you buy something at a bargain price. The phrase used in this dialogue costa di meno, literally 'it costs less', is very often used. It's therefore better to ask costa di meno il biglietto per l'espresso? 'is the ticket for the espresso cheaper?' or literally 'does the ticket for the espresso cost less?'

There is or there are?

In Italian, as in English, the phrase c'è means: 'there is', whilst if it's more than one choice, you say ci sono, 'there are' as in ci sono due treni 'there are two trains. These are very idiomatic expressions and you hear them a lot.

Well, let me think about it

We have already come across words that buy you a bit of time before making a statement such as beh and mah (both meaning 'well'). Here we find another word dunque ('so', 'therefore') doing much the same thing. Again, it means 'well' but it's rather a 'let's see' allowing the ticket man a bit of time before he gives the train information to Anna.

A ticket to where?

When you ask for a ticket to somewhere, you use the article per to mean 'to'. When asking about the arrival times, you say a: a Venezia, a Roma, a Milano.

Give us a discount!

The man asks Anna if she qualifies for qualche sconto 'any discount'. The word sconto is very useful as is the phrase mi da uno sconto? 'will you give me a discount?' If you go round an Italian market with someone who likes to haggle, this is what you'll hear them use. Did you notice that the article is uno, not un as you might expect, this is because the word starts with sc-, which is one of the s + consonant combinations which require uno and lo as the singular articles, and gli for the plural: gli sconti.

did you know ...?

When travelling by train in Italy

You must validate (convalidare) your ticket before you get on. The orange validating machines are situated at platform entrances or there is a special slot in automatic ticket machines which allows you to validate your ticket as soon as you've bought it. It also applies for the return leg of the journey when the ticket must be validated again.

Time and money

We've shown how times and sums of money are written out. The train times are given in the 24-hour clock with e 'and' to separate hours and minutes: 16 e tre '16 and three' in other words 'three minutes past four' (pm). When written, a colon separates the hours from the minutes, 16:03. Another thing to watch out for is the way the full stop and comma are used differently in Italian. A full stop, rather than a comma, is used in Italian thousand numbers, while a comma rather than a full stop is used in decimals. So, the price of your ticket is €49,42 (forty nine euros and forty two cents), but the price of your holiday could be €1.200 (one thousand two hundred euros) or even €1.200,50 (one thousand two hundred euros and fifty cents).

now practise

> understanding railway announcements

extra vocabulary

the train leaves at ...
il treno parte alle ...
eel ***tren****-o* ***par****-tay* ***al****-lay ...*

the film starts at ...
il film comincia alle ...
*eel feelm ko-****meentch****-a* ***al****-lay ...*

at one o'clock
all'una
*al-****loo****-na*

at two thirty
alle due e mezza
al*-lay* ***doo****-ay ay* ***med****-dza*

at 1600 hours
alle sedici
al*-lay* ***sed****-ee-tchee*

at five to five
alle cinque meno cinque
al*-lay* ***tcheen****-kway* ***men****-o* ***tcheen****-kway*

at a quarter to eight
alle otto meno un quarto
al*-lay* ***ot****-to* ***men****-o oon* ***kwart****-o*

at twenty to seven
alle sette meno venti
al*-lay* ***set****-tay* ***men****-o ven-tee*

at midnight
a mezzanotte
a ***med****-dza-****not****-tay*

at midday
a mezzogiorno
a ***med****-dzo-****djor****-no*

at 20.40
alle venti e quaranta
al*-lay* ***ven****-tee ay kwa-ran-****ta***

Catching a bus

get to know ...

> **ago**
> **sapere and conoscere**
> **irregular verbs**
> **buses**

Franco **Mi scusi, signora, è questa la fermata dell'autobus che porta in centro?**
*mee **skoo**-zee seen-**yo**-ra, ay **kwes**-ta la fer-**ma**-ta del-**laoo**-to-boos kay **por**-ta een **tchen**-tro?*
Excuse me, is this the stop for the bus that goes into the town centre?

Sig.ra Sala **Sì, è questa. Può prendere il numero quindici oppure il quarantasei**
*see, ay **kwes**-ta. pwo **pren**-der-ay eel **noo**-mer-o **kween**-deetch-ee op-**poo**-ray eel kwa-ran-ta-**say**-ee*
Yes it is. You can get the number fifteen or the forty six

Franco **Passano di frequente, che lei sappia?**
***pas**-san-o dee frek-**wen**-tay, kay lay **sap**-pya?*
Do they go often, as far as you know?

Sig.ra Sala **Sì, passano ogni dieci minuti**
*see, pas-**san**-o **on**-yee **dyetch**-ee mee-**noo**-tee*
Yes, there's one every ten minutes

Franco **I biglietti si possono comprare sull'autobus?**
*ee beel-**yet**-tee see pos-**so**-no kom-**pra**-ray sool-**aoo**-to-boos?*
Can you buy tickets on the bus?

Sig.ra Sala **No, li deve comprare all'edicola e costano un euro**
*no, lee **dev**-ay kom-**prar**-ay al-led-**ee**-ko-la ay **kos**-tan-o oon **ay**-oo-ro*
No, you have to get them at the news-stand and they cost one euro

(on board)

Franco **Scusi, il biglietto va timbrato?**
***skoo**-zee eel beel-**yet**-to va teem-**brat**-o?*
Excuse me, does the ticket have to be stamped?

Passenger **Sì, e dura settantacinque minuti dalla prima convalida**
*see, ay **doo**-ra set-tan-ta-**tcheen**-kway mee-**noo**-tee **dal**-la **pree**-ma kon-**val**-ee-da*
Yes, and it's valid for seventy five minutes from the first time it's stamped

Franco **Questo autobus passa davanti all'ufficio turistico?**
***kwest**-o **aoo**-to-boos **pas**-sa da-**van**-tee al-loo-**feetch**-o too-**rees**-tee-ko?*
Does this bus go past the tourist office?

Passenger **Sì, scenda alla fermata davanti alla stazione**
*see, **shen**-da **al**-la fer-**ma**-ta da-**van**-tee **al**-la stats-**yo**-nay*
Yes, get off at the stop in front of the station

Franco **Mi può dire, per favore, quando devo scendere? Non conosco bene la città**
*me pwo **dee**-ray, payr fa-**vor**-ay **kwand**-o **dev**-o **shen**-der-ay? non kon-**os**-ko **ben**-ay la **tcheet**-ta*
Can you tell me when I have to get off? I don't know the town very well

Passenger **Sì, va bene. Si accomodi vicino a me e le dirò dove scendere**
*see, va **ben**-ay. see ak-**ko**-mod-ee veetch-**een**-o a may ay lay **dee**-ro **dov**-ay **shen**-der-ay*
Yes, of course. Sit by me and I'll tell you where you have to get off

Franco **Grazie, molto gentile**
***grats**-yay, **molt**-o djen-**tee**-lay*
Thank you, that's very kind of you

from the dialogue

la fermata dell'autobus
*la fer-**ma**-ta del-**laoo**-to-boos*
the bus stop

può prendere ...
*pwo **pren**-der-ay ...*
you can get ...

passano di frequente
***pas**-san-o dee frek-**wen**-tay*
do they go often

ogni dieci minuti
***on**-yee **dyetch**-ee mee-**noo**-tee*
every ten minutes

all'edicola
*al-led-**ee**-ko-la*
at the news-stand

davanti alla stazione
*da-**van**-tee al-la stats-**yo**-nay*
in front of the station

mi può dire?
*me pwo **dee**-ray*
can you tell me?

molto gentile
***molt**-o djen-**tee**-lay*
that's very kind

What do you know?

Franco asks if the buses go by often, che lei sappia 'as far as you know'. This is a form of the verb sapere which means 'to know' when it is a case of factual knowledge: so che ti piace 'I know you like it', so che Roma è in Italia 'I know Rome is in Italy'. You will often hear sì, lo so 'yes, I know', or non lo sapevo 'I didn't know'. When know is followed by 'why', 'where', 'what', 'how', etc, it is translated by sapere: non so dov'è la stazione 'I don't know where the station is', sa quanto costa? 'do you know how much it costs?' You must also use sapere when it expresses the idea of being able or not able to do something, as in non so guidare 'I can't drive' in other words, I don't know how to drive. Or Paul non sa nuotare 'Paul can't swim', in other words Paul doesn't know how to swim. When it is a case of knowing places or people, however, the verb conoscere is used. Lo conosco molto bene 'I know him very well', la conosco da due anni 'I've known her for two years'. Franco, who is a stranger in town, says non conosco bene la città 'I don't know the town very well'.

Able and willing

In Italian the verbs potere 'to be able to' and dovere 'to have to' are very useful for giving advice and information. They always come before an infinitive as in può prendere ... 'you can take ...', or li deve comprare 'you have to buy them'. These verbs are also helpful when you need to ask for something as in mi può dire per favore? 'can you tell me, please?' The phrase mi può ...? is a nice polite way of asking for just about anything: mi può spiegare? 'can you explain?', mi può auitare? 'can you help me?', mi può dare ...? 'can you give me ...?'. This answer may be deve ... as in deve prendere l'autobus o la metropolitana 'you have to take the bus or the underground.

> Potere and Dovere RefZone 29, 31.

Passing by

The bus 'goes' or 'runs' every so often in English. But in Italian it 'passes'. Passano di frequente? 'do they go by often?' – sì, passano ogni dieci minuti 'yes they run every ten minutes'. Note that the verb passare is also a common way of saying that you are popping in to see someone or dropping by. So passo da te fra dieci minuti means 'I'll pop in to see you in ten minutes'.

On and off, up and down

In Italian you 'get up onto' (salire su) and 'get down from' (scendere da) the bus, much as in English we get 'on' and 'off'. It's the same for trains and planes – and automobiles too. In Italian you salire in macchina 'get into a car' and scendere da 'get out' of it. A relic of the early days of motoring, where some real climbing up and down was required!

Highly irregular

Unfortunately for us English-speakers, some of the commonest and most useful verbs in Italian are irregular, which means that one form can look very different from another – posso, può, possono are all present forms of the verb potere 'to be able to' and so and sappia are forms of the verb sapere 'to know'. Because you will hear them so often, the best thing to do is to study the verb tables and learn them by heart.

extra vocabulary

the bus station
la stazione delle autolinee
*la stats-**yo**-nay **del**-lay aoot-o-**lee**-nay-ay*

bus number 9
l'autobus numero nove
***laoot**-o-boos **noo**-mer-o **nov**-ay*

to catch the bus
prendere l'autobus
***pren**-der-ay **laoot**-o-boos*

to get on the bus
salire sull'autobus
*sa-**lee**-ray sool-**laoot**-o-boos*

to get off the bus
scendere dall'autobus
***shen**-der-ay dal-**laoot**-o-boos*

do you go to the station?
va alla stazione?
*va **al**-la stats-**yo**-nay?*

the coach
la corriera
*la korr-**yer**-a*

how long does it take?
quanto ci mette?
***kwant**-o tchee **met**-tay?*

did you know ...?

Once you have bought your bus ticket, either from the edicola 'newspaper kiosk' or from a bar, you must remember to stamp it in the machine on the bus. This is called convalida and once it's stamped you can travel for a certain period of time (usually 75 minutes). Incidentally if you are going to stay in town for a couple of days or more, it's worth buying a carta turistica which is cheaper and allows unlimited travel for its duration. You can get from an Unfficio Turistico or Azienda Turistica, your friendly local tourist office.

> sapere and conoscere

An internet café

get to know ...

- subject pronouns
- email addresses
- emphatic pronouns
- internet vocabulary

Nadia **Silvia, sai dove c'è un punto Internet dalle tue parti? Devo confermare via e-mail una riunione per la prossima settimana**
__seelv__-ya, saee __dov__-ay tchay oon __poon__-to __een__-ter-net __dal__-lay __too__-ay __par__-tee? __dev__-o kon-fer-__ma__-ray __vee__-a __ee__-mel __oo__-na ree-oon-__yo__-nay payr la __pros__-see-ma set-tee-__ma__-na
Silvia, do you know where there's an internet café near you? I have to send an email to confirm a meeting next week

Silvia **Ma sì, non ci sono problemi. Ce n'è uno proprio dietro l'angolo. Ti accompagno io**
ma see, non tchee __so__-no prob-__lem__-ee. tchay nay __oo__-no __prop__-ree-o __dyet__-ro __lan__-gol-o. tee ak-kom-__pan__-yo __ee__-o
Sure, it's no problem. There's one just round the corner. I'll come with you

Nadia **Tu sai quanto costa connettersi?**
too saee __kwant__-o __kos__-ta kon-__net__-ter-see?
Do you know how much it costs to go online?

Silvia **Credo che sia cinque euro all'ora. A proposito, non ho il tuo indirizzo e-mail. Me lo daresti, per favore?**
__kred__-o kay __see__-a __tcheen__-kway __ay__-oo-ro al-__lor__-a. a prop-__oz__-ee-to, non o eel __too__-o een-dee-__reets__-o __ee__-mel. me lo da-__res__-tee, payr fa-__vor__-ay?
I think it's five euros an hour. By the way, I haven't got your email address. Will you give it to me please?

Nadia **Sì, come no ... è nadia quattro chiocciola tiscalinet punto eet. E qual è il tuo indirizzo di posta elettronica?**
see, __kom__-ay no ... ay __nad__-ya __kwat__-tro kee-__otch__-o-la __tee__-ska-lee-net __poont__-o eet. ay kwal ay eel __too__-o een-dee-__reets__-o dee __pos__-ta el-et-__tron__-ee-ka?
Yes, of course ... it's nadia4@tiscalinet.it. And what's your email address?

Silvia **Il mio è silvia punto rossi chiocciola fiat punto eet. Questo è il mio indirizzo dell'ufficio. Non ne ho uno personale. Il sito è voo voo voo punto fiat punto eet (www.fiat.it). Beh, andiamo!**
*eel **mee**-o ay **seelv**-ya **poont**-o **ros**-see kee-**otch**-o-la **fee**-at **poont**-o eet. **kwest**-o ay eel **mee**-o een-dee-**reets**-o del-loof-**fee**-tcho. non nay o **oo**-no per-son-**a**-lay. eel **see**-to ay voo voo voo **poont**-o **fee**-at **poont**-o eet. bay, and-**ya**-mo!*
Mine's silvia.rossi@fiat.it. That's my office address. I haven't got a personal one. The site is www dot fiat dot it. Right then, let's go!

Somewhere nearby

In Italian, the phrase dalle tue parti is not easily translated. It means in your area or neighbourhood. You will hear this expression quite often: c'è un buon ristorante (or whatever) dalle tue parti? 'is there a good restaurant in your area?' It's a friendly way of finding out about someone else's neck of the woods.

Where it's @

E-mail addresses are international and very straightforward in writing, but you may find yourself needing to read one out aloud, at which point you will need to know the conventional pronunciation of the various bits. That squiggle we call an 'at' sign, is chiocciola (*kee-**otch**-o-la*) literally 'snail': while the 'dot' is punto. The www part in Italian is nice and easy: voo voo voo. So the address www.collins.co.uk would be voo voo voo collins punto chee o punto oo kappa (where co and uk are both spelt out).

from the dialogue

sai dove c'è ...?
*saee **dov**-ay tchay ...?*
do you know where there's ...?

dalle tue parti
*__dal__-lay **too**-ay **par**-tee*
near you

una riunione
*__oo__-na ree-oon-**yo**-nay*
a meeting

la prossima settimana
*la **pros**-see-ma set-tee-**ma**-na*
next week

non ci sono problemi
*non tchee **so**-no prob-**lem**-ee*
it's no problem

credo che sia ...
*__kred__-o kay **see**-a*
I think it's ...

cinque euro all'ora
*__tcheen__-kway **ay**-oo-ro al-**lor**-a*
5 euros per hour

a proposito
*a prop-**oz**-ee-to*
by the way

non ho il tuo indirizzo
*non o eel **too**-o een-dee-**reets**-o*
I don't have your address

Do we need them, or don't we?

In English, a verb is always preceded by a pronoun (I, you, he, etc) and it tells us clearly who's doing what. In Italian there is no great need to include the pronoun because the ending of the verb already spells out who's doing what. In this dialogue you have sai dove? 'do you know where?' and devo confermare 'I have to confirm' where the pronoun has not been used. But again you have tu, sai quanto costa? 'do you know how much it is? and ti accompagno io 'I'll go with you'. In these cases Nadia and Silvia have decided to include tu and io as a way of emphasizing what they are saying. The choice is yours – you can use the pronouns if you feel the need to make something clearer or more emphatic. > PRONOUNS REFZONE 19.

Needing ne

In Italian we've seen ne 'of them' used very often. And whereas in English it may only be implied, in Italian it's always needed. So when Nadia asks if there's an internet café nearby, Silvia's reply is ce n'è uno proprio dietro l'angolo 'there's one just around the corner' where the ne means 'of them', but which you wouldn't bother to say in English. If you were being asked how many children you have quanti figli hai? the answer could be ne ho tre 'I have three (of them)'. If you don't use the ne, you'll have to repeat figli – ho tre figli. And if you had none you can say non ne ho 'I don't have any (of them)' or you'd have to repeat the figli, non ho figli. Using ne makes your Italian sound much more fluent!

Me ...

Except for a few exceptions the definite article is used for 'my', 'your' etc: il mio indirizzo e-mail, il tuo indirizzo di posta elettronica, il suo amico, la sua amica. These are possessive adjectives and agree with the noun they go with. Il suo amico means either 'his friend', or 'her friend' – suo is masculine because the friend in question is male. In the same way la sua amica means either 'his friend' or 'her friend' – we need to know the context to know which it is – all we can tell from the phrase is that the friend is female. With a bit more context all becomes clear: Katy e la sua amica 'Katy and her (female) friend', Katy e il suo amico 'Katy and her (male) friend.

... and mine

Il mio, la mia, il tuo, la tua, etc are also used to mean 'mine' and 'yours': ecco il mio indirizzo, qual'è il tuo? 'here's my address, what's yours?', di chi è quella macchina? è la mia 'whose is that car? it's mine'. > POSSESSIVES REFZONE 13.

Nuovo messaggio

a: d.fede@montessori.it

da: nadia4@tiscalinet.it

oggetto: riunione

cc:

ccn:

Buongiorno,

vi invio questo messaggio per confermare che sarò presente alla riunione di martedì 17 alle ore 15:00 presso i vostri uffici.

Cordiali saluti

Nadia Brambilla

Hello

I am sending this message to confirm that I will attend the meeting on Tuesday 17 at 3 o'clock at your offices.

best regards

Nadia Brambilla

now practise

> **emphatic pronouns**

extra vocabulary

to write a letter
scrivere una lettera
skree-ver-ay oo-na let-ter-a

to send an email
mandare un e-mail
man-da-ray oon ee-mel

to receive a fax
ricevere un fax
reetch-ev-er-ay oon faks

to text
mandare un SMS
man-da-ray oon ess-em-es-say

a search engine
un motore di ricerca
oon mot-or-ay dee ree-tcher-ka

website
sito web
seet-o web

my address
il mio indirizzo
eel mee-o een-dee-reets-tso

my mobile
il mio cellulare
eel mee-o tchel-loo-la-ray

Booking a hotel

get to know ...

- > **future**
- > **dates**
- > **writing letters**

Caroline **Pronto? Albergo La Luna?**
***pront**-o? al-**ber**-go la **loo**-na?*
Hello? Is that the La Luna hotel?

Receptionist **Sì, dica?**
*see, **dee**-ka?*
Yes, can I help you?

Caroline **Vorrei prenotare una camera per tre notti, dal quindici al diciassette agosto**
*vor-**ray**-ee pren-ot-**a**-ray **oo**-na **ka**-mer-a payr tray **not**-tee, dal **kween**-deetch-ee al deetch-as-**set**-tay a-**gost**-o*
I'd like to book a room for three nights, from the fifteenth to the seventeenth of August

Receptionist **Un momento per favore ... Sì, non c'è problema, che tipo di camera desidera?**
*oon mo-**ment**-o payr fa-**vor**-ay ... see, non tchay prob-**lem**-a, kay **tee**-po dee **ka**-mer-a dez-**ee**-der-a?*
One moment please ... Yes, that's no problem, what kind of room would you like?

Caroline **Vorrei una camera singola con bagno**
*vor-**ray**-ee **oo**-na ka-**mer**-a **seen**-go-la kon **ban**-yo*
I'd like a single room with a bath

Receptionist **Mi dispiace, abbiamo soltanto una singola con doccia. Se vuole, può prenotare una doppia con bagno, ma costa di più. Viene quarantasei euro per notte, mentre una singola costa trentacinque euro**
*mee dees-**pyatch**-ay, ab-**ya**-mo sol-**tant**-o **oo**-na **seen**-go-la kon **dotch**-tcha. say **vwol**-ay, pwo pren-ot-**a**-ray **oo**-na **dop**-pya kon **ban**-yo, ma **kos**-ta dee pyoo. **vyen**-ay kwar-an-ta-**say** **ay**-oo-ro payr **not**-tay, **men**-tray **oo**-na **seen**-go-la **kos**-ta tren-ta-**tcheen**-kway **eoo**-ro*
I'm sorry, we've only got a single with a shower. If you want you can book a double with a bath, but it costs more. It costs 46 euros a night whereas a single costs 35 euros

Caroline **No, grazie, prendo la singola con doccia**
*no **grats**-yay, **prend**-o la **seen**-go-la kon **dotch**-tcha*
No thanks, I'll take the single with a shower

Receptionist **Bene, mi può dare il suo nome e indirizzo?**
***ben**-ay, mee pwo **da**-ray eel **soo**-o **nom**-ay ay een-dee-**reet**-so?*
That's fine, can you give me your name and address?

Caroline **Sì, mi chiamo Caroline Smartt. Si scrive S, M, A, R, doppia T. Abito al numero venti di Orchard Lane, a Oxford. Il codice postale è OX1 3PN**
*see, mee **kyam**-o ka-ro-**laeen** smart. see **skree**-vay **es**-say, **em**-may, a, **er**-ray, **dop**-pya tay. **a**-bee-to al **noo**-mer-o **ven**-tee dee **or**-tchard layn, a **oks**-ford. eel **kod**-eetch-ay pos-**ta**-lay ay o, eeks **oo**-no tray pay **en**-nay*
Yes, my name's Caroline Smartt. That's spelled S,M,A,R,double T. I live at number 20 Orchard Lane, Oxford. The postcode is OX1 3PN

Receptionist **La ringrazio. Mi può inviare una lettera di conferma o un fax ed un acconto di cinquanta euro?**
*la reen-**grats**-yo. mee pwo een-vee-**a**-ray **oo**-na let-**ter**-a dee kon-**fer**-ma o oon faks ed oon ak-**kont**-o dee tcheen-**kwan**-ta **ay**-oo-ro?*
Thank you. Could you please send me a letter or fax to confirm, and a deposit of 50 euros?

Caroline **Sì, certo, glieli manderò entro una settimana. E scusi, posso pagare l'acconto con la mia carta di credito?**
*see, **tchert**-o, **lyel**-ee man-der-**o** **en**-tro **oo**-na set-tee-**ma**-na. ay **skoo**-zee, **pos**-so pa-**ga**-ray lak-**kont**-o kon la **mee**-a **kar**-ta dee **kred**-eet-o?*
Yes, of course. I'll send you them within the next week. Just one more thing, can I pay the bill with my credit card?

Receptionist **Sì, certamente, metta il numero e la data di scadenza della carta di credito nella lettera**
*see, tcher-ta-**men**-tay, **met**-ta eel **noo**-mer-o ay la **da**-ta dee skad-**ent**-sa **del**-la **kar**-ta dee **kred**-eet-o **nel**-la **let**-ter-a*
Yes, certainly, put the credit card number and expiry date in your letter

Caroline **Grazie mille. A presto**
***grats**-yay **meel**-lay. a **prest**-o*
Many thanks. See you soon

Receptionist **Arrivederla, signora Smartt**
*ar-ree-ved-**er**-la, seen-**yo**-ra smart*
Goodbye Mrs Smartt

from the dialogue

pronto?
***pront**-o?*
hello?

prenotare una camera
*pren-ot-**a**-ray **oo**-na **ka**-mer-a*
to book a room

per tre notti
*payr tray **not**-tee*
for three nights

se vuole
*say **vwol**-ay*
if you want

costa di più
*ma **kos**-ta dee pyoo*
it costs more

il suo nome
*eel **soo**-o **nom**-ay*
your name

si scrive ...
*see **skree**-vay ...*
it's spelt ...

il codice postale
*eel **kod**-eetch-ay pos-**ta**-lay*
the postcode

una lettera di conferma
***oo**-na let-**ter**-a dee kon-**fer**-ma*
a confirmation letter

un acconto
*oon ak-**kont**-o*
a deposit

entro una settimana
***en**-tro **oo**-na set-tee-**ma**-na*
within a week

la data di scadenza
*la **da**-ta dee skad-**ent**-sa*
the expiry date

a presto
*a **prest**-o*
see you soon

28

Spelling in towns

When giving or receiving unfamiliar names verbally, you will naturally want to spell them out. Use the verb scrivere 'to write' – si scrive ... 'it's written/spelt ...' For double letters, you just say doppia 'double'. In Italian to make it very clear you can use the name of a town that begins with the letter that you are spelling. This is known as l'alfabeto telefonico 'the telephone alphabet'. The towns normally used are: Ancona, Bologna, Como, Domodossola, Empoli, Firenze, Genova, Hotel, Imola, Livorno, Milano, Napoli, Orvieto, Pisa, Quebec, Roma, Salerno, Torino, Udine, Venezia, Zara. Letters that are not really 'native' to Italian are j, which in Italian is i lunga (ee *loon*-ga), k = kappa (*kap*-pa), w = doppia v (v is pronounced *voo*), x = ics (eeks) and y = ipsilon (eep-see-lon) or i greca. (ee *grek*-a). So if you are spelling SMITH you could simply say Salerno – Milano – Imola – Torino – Hotel.

It'll cost you

Apart from just saying that something 'is' a certain price, you can use the verb costare 'to cost' as in this dialogue ma costa di più 'but it costs more'. Another verb for indicating a price is venire 'to come' as in 'it comes to'. The phrase viene 46 euro per notte can be translated 'it comes to 46 euros per night'.

The dating game

Here is another little stress-saver – dates are given without the 'th' part in Italian, so not the sixteenth of September but the sixteen September, or as here dal quindici al diciassette agosto (from the 15th to the 17th of August). However the first of the month is an exception. On this particular day, it's not 'one' but 'the first'. So the first of January is il primo gennaio, where primo can be written as 1°.

> MONTHS AND SEASONS REFZONE 7.

The other way round

Italians put the street number after the street name: via Aurelia 123 and the codice postale 'postcode' before the town 00100 ROMA.

Back to the future

In Italian you can often use the present tense when talking about what you are going to do: ti accompagno io 'I'll go with you', vado a Milano fra due giorni 'I'm going to Milan in two days'. There is however a future tense, glieli manderò entro una settimana 'I'll send you them within a week'. The accent on the end of manderò shows that the stress comes on the final syllable. All the 'I' futures end in ò: manderò, andrò 'I will go', parlerò 'I will speak'. All the 'he/she/it' endings end in à: manderà, andrà, parlerà. If you want to add to your list of ways to ask the price, you could add another – quanto costerà 'how much will it cost?'

Further to

In seguito a is a very common way of introducing a subject in a letter: literally 'following on from ...' and perhaps best translated as 'with regard to...'. You'll notice if you read any formal letters in Italian that the ending is much more verbose and formal than the English 'yours faithfully' or 'yours sincerely'. There may be long phrases such as La prego di accettare i miei più cordiali saluti and so on and so forth – there are several possible variations on this theme. However, things are getting shorter, even in Italian. So you can safely open a business letter with far fewer words – Gentile Signor Direttore 'Dear Sir' – and close with Cordiali saluti 'best regards'.

Spettabile Direzione
Albergo 'La Luna'
via Aurelia 123
00100 Roma

Oxford, 3 luglio 2005 (3 July)

Gentile Signor Direttore (Dear Sir)

In seguito alla mia telefonata (Further to my phone call) *le confermo la prenotazione* (I'm writing to confirm my reservation) *di una camera singola con doccia per tre notti* (of a single room with shower, for three nights) *dal 15 al 17 di agosto* (from the 15-17 August).

Le mando pure i dati della mia carta di credito (I also enclose the details of my credit card) *come pagamento per un acconto di 50 euro* (as payment for a deposit of 50 euros)

Cordiali saluti (Yours faithfully)
Caroline Smartt

extra vocabulary

a single room
una camera singola
***oo**-na **ka**-mer-a **seen**-go-la*

a double room
una camera doppia
***oo**-na **ka**-mer-a **dop**-pya*

a room for three
una camera per tre
***oo**-na **ka**-mer-a payr tray*

a family room
una camera familiare
***oo**-na **ka**-mer-a fa-meel-**ya**-ray*

with double bed
con letto matrimoniale
*kon **let**-to ma-tree-mon-**ya**-lay*

with twin beds
con due letti
*kon **doo**-ay **let**-tee*

with bunk beds
con letti a castelli
*kon **let**-tee a kas-**tel**-lee*

a cot
un lettino
*oon let-**teen**-o*

for one night
per una notte
*payr **oo**-na **not**-tay*

from 4 to 8 July
dal quattro all'otto luglio
*dal **kwat**-tro al-**lot**-to **lool**-yo*

for Friday night
per venerdì sera
*payr ven-er-**dee** **ser**-a*

now practise

> **spelling aloud**

Not feeling well

get to know ...

> **illness**
> **reflexive verbs**
> **adverbs of time**
> **commands**

Mario **Pronto, Carla? Allora ci si vede stasera al ristorante?**
***pront**-o, **kar**-la? al-**lor**-a tchee see **ved**-ay sta-**ser**-a al reest-o-**ran**-tay?*
Hello, Carla? So are we seeing each other tonight at the restaurant?

Carla **Mi spiace, ma penso di non poter venire. Non mi sento tanto bene**
*mee **spyatch**-ay, ma **pen**-so dee non po-**ter** ven-**ee**-ray. non mee **sent**-o **tant**-o **ben**-ay*
I'm sorry, but I don't think I can come. I don't feel very well

Mario **Ahi, mi dispiace. Che cos'hai?**
*aee, mee dees-**pyatch**-ay. kay koz-**aee**?*
Oh, I'm sorry. What's wrong with you?

Carla **Ho mal di testa e di gola e forse anche un po' di febbre**
*o mal dee **tes**-ta ay dee **gol**-a ay **for**-say **an**-kay oon po dee **feb**-bray*
I've got a headache, a sore throat, and maybe a slight temperature too

Mario **Pensi di avere l'influenza?**
***pen**-see dee a-**ver**-ay leen-floo-**ents**-a?*
Do you think you've got flu?

Carla **Può darsi. Adesso vado in farmacia a chiedere consiglio al farmacista**
*pwo **dar**-see. a-**des**-so **vad**-o een far-match-**ee**-a a **kyed**-er-ay kon-**seel**-yo al far-match-**ees**-ta*
Maybe I have. I'm going to go to the chemist's to ask the pharmacist for advice

Mario **Vuoi che venga con te?**
*vwoy kay **ven**-ga kon tay?*
Do you want me to come with you?

Carla **Grazie, sei gentile, ma ci vado subito, così poi posso andare a letto**
***grats**-yay, say djen-**tee**-lay, ma tchee **vad**-o **soo**-beet-o, **ko**-zee pwoy **pos**-so an-**da**-ray a **let**-to*
Thank you, that's very nice of you, but I'm going there right now, so that I can go to bed straight after

Mario **OK. Allora riposati. Ti chiamo domani per sapere se stai meglio**
*o-**kay**. al-**lor**-a ree-**poz**-a-tee. tee **kyam**-o dom-**a**-nee payr sa-**per**-ay say staee **mel**-yo*
Okay. Go to bed then (rest yourself). I'll call you tomorrow to find out if you're better

Carla **Grazie e scusa ancora per stasera. Sarà per la prossima volta**
***grats**-yay ay **skoo**-za an-**kor**-a payr sta-**ser**-a. sa-**ra** payr la **pros**-see-ma **vol**-ta*
Thank you, and sorry again about this evening. We'll go another time (it'll be for another time)

Mario **Non preoccuparti e curati! Ciao**
*non pray-ok-koo-**par**-tee ay koo-**ra**-tee! tchao*
Don't worry, and take care of yourself. Bye

OK, all right, agreed?

How do you ask if things are OK? Well, the word OK is often used in informal Italian as we see in this dialogue. You'll probably be familiar with the informal expression va bene? 'OK' or 'are you OK?' The reply could be: sì, va bene or mica male 'not too bad' or non c'è male literally 'there's nothing bad', or simply, OK.

How do you feel?

Non mi sento tanto bene, says Carla – literally 'I don't feel myself very well'. When describing how you feel in Italian you need to use this 'reflexive' construction. Reflexive verbs are used when the action is considered to be done to oneself (to wash yourself, to enjoy yourself), even when there doesn't seem to be any logic in it. Another example of this cropped up in the restaurant when the waiter said si accomodi literally 'take yourself a seat' or more naturally 'do take a seat'. Other examples with sentirsi 'to feel' might include mi sento un po' debole 'I feel rather weak' or Sara si sente in forma 'Sara feels on top form'.

from the dialogue

ci si vede stasera?
*tchee see **ved**-ay sta-**ser**-a?*
are we seeing each other tonight?

non mi sento tanto bene
*non mee **sent**-o **tant**-o **ben**-ay*
I don't feel very well

che cos'hai?
*kay koz-**aee**?*
what's wrong?

ho mal di testa
*oh mal dee **tes**-ta*
I've got a headache

un po' di febbre
*oon po dee **feb**-bray*
a slight temperature

può darsi
*pwo **dar**-see*
maybe

a chiedere consiglio
*a **kyed**-er-ay kon-**seel**-yo*
to ask for advice

ci vado subito
*tchee **vad**-o **soo**-beet-o*
I'm going there right now

andare a letto
*an-**da**-ray a **let**-to*
to go to bed

ti chiamo domani
*tee **kyam**-o dom-**a**-nee*
I'll call you tomorrow

la prossima volta
*la **pros**-see-ma **vol**-ta*
next time

non preoccuparti
*non pray-ok-koo-**par**-tee*
don't worry

A pain in the ...

In English we have a multitude of ways of saying we're unwell: you might have a headache, or a sore throat or a painful toe. The key term in Italian is mal di 'pain of' with the verb avere 'to have' plus whichever part of the body that is hurting. So ho mal di gola literally 'I have pain of throat', but more naturally 'I have a sore throat', Marco ha mal di testa 'Marco has a headache'. When talking about illness in English we often omit the definite article: 'have you got flu?' 'she has chickenpox', but it needs to be included in Italian: hai l'influenza? ha la varicella.

Going places

How do you say that you are going to a certain shop or place? Vado in farmacia says Carla, but she could have used a construction involving da and the person who owns the shop or place. Hence you say vado dal farmacista 'I'm going to see the pharmacist' or devo andare dal dentista 'I have to go to the dentist's'. Remember that da goes with the person: da Maria 'at Maria's' and in goes with the actual place: vado in banca 'I'm off to the bank', vado in bagno, 'I'm going to the bathroom'.

Do's and dont's

When giving instructions or commands you use the 'imperative' form of the verb, which has different endings according to who you're talking to (formal or informal). Here we see the tu imperative form of a reflexive verb, curarsi 'to look after oneself': curati! 'look after yourself!', and another in the negative: non preoccuparti! 'don't worry!' In the negative tu imperative, you use the infinitive: non andare 'don't go'. When it's a reflexive verb, then the infinitive loses the final -e and the pronoun is tacked on the end: non preoccuparti.

> Verbs RefZone 20.

Pronto

This is what you say when answering the phone. It literally means 'ready' and is an adjective. However, used in the phone context, it doesn't change, both men and women say pronto (not pronta). You give your name after sono ... 'I am ...' rather than 'it is ...' as we say in English.

When's it going to be?

It is important to establish when things are happening, or when they have happened. The key words are oggi 'today', domani 'tomorrow', ieri 'yesterday', adesso 'now' and subito 'straight away'. The sta- on some such words is what's left of (que)sta 'this' so stamattina means 'this morning', stasera means 'this evening'. All these words make it clear when things are happening: adesso vado in farmacia 'I'm off to the chemist's now', ti chiamo domani 'I'll call you tomorrow', ci vado subito 'I'm going straight away' and ci si vede stasera? 'are we going to see each other this evening?'. With these time words, Italian very often uses the present tense.

extra vocabulary

I have stomachache
ho mal di stomaco
*o mal dee **sto**-ma-ko*

my back hurts
ho mal di schiena
*o mal dee **skyen**-a*

she has earache
ha mal d'orecchio
*a mal dor-**ek**-kyo*

he has toothache
ha mal di denti
*a mal dee **den**-tee*

do you feel ill?
ti senti male?
*tee **sen**-tee **ma**-lay?*

I'm pregnant
sono incinta
***so**-no een-**tcheen**-ta*

he has high blood pressure
ha la pressione alta
*a la pres-**syo**-nay **al**-ta*

she's diabetic
è diabetica
*ay dee-a-**bet**-ee-ka*

I've cut myself
mi sono tagliato(a)
*mee **so**-no tal-**yat**-o(a)*

she had a fall
è caduta
*ay ka-**doo**-ta*

> aches and pains

A visit to London

get to know ...

- > **informal Italian**
- > **past participles**
- > **avere and essere**

Dario **Ciao Vito, ciao Grusci. È molto tempo che non ci si vede. Ma dove vi siete cacciati?**
*tchao **vee**-to, tchao **groo**-shee. ay **molt**-o a **tem**-po kay non tchee see **ved**-ay. ma **dov**-ay vee **syet**-ay katch-**tcha**-tee?*
Hi Vito, hi Grusci. We haven't seen each other for ages – where have you been hiding yourselves?

Vito **Eravamo in quel di Londra. Abbiamo fatto un bel ponte!**
*er-a-**va**-mo een kwel dee **lon**-dra. ab-**ya**-mo **fat**-to oon bel **pon**-tay!*
We've been off in London. We had a great long weekend

Grusci **Londra era stupenda. Mi è piaciuta molto**
***lon**-dra **ay**-ra stoo-**pen**-da. mee ay pyatch-**oo**-ta **molt**-o*
London was fantastic. I really liked it

Dario **Ma no! E cosa avete fatto di bello?**
*ma no! ay **ko**-za a-**vet**-ay **fat**-to dee **bel**-lo?*
Wow! Did you do anything interesting?

Vito **L'abbiamo girata in lungo e in largo. Abbiamo preso gli autobus a due piani, la metro e abbiamo camminato!**
*lab-**ya**-mo djee-**ra**-ta een **loon**-go ay een **lar**-go. ab-**ya**-mo **pray**-zo lyee **aoo**-to-boos a **doo**-ay **pyan**-ee, la **met**-ro ay ab-**ya**-mo kam-mee-**na**-to!*
We went all over the place. We look double-decker buses, the tube – and we walked!

Grusci **Eh, sì. Siamo stati dallo zio di Vito. Sai, lui si è trasferito a Londra vent'anni fa**
*eh, see. **syam**-o **sta**-tee **dal**-lo **dzee**-o dee **veet**-o. saee, **loo**-ee see ay tras-fer-**eet**-o a **lon**-dra **ven**-tan-nee fa*
Yes, We stayed with Vito's uncle. You know, he moved to London twenty years ago

Dario **Ma il mangiare, com'era? Uno schifo, no?**
*ma eel man-**dja**-ray, kom-**er**-a? **oo**-no **skee**-fo, no?*
What was the food like? I bet it was rubbish, wasn't it?

Vito **Figurati! C'era di tutto. Abbiamo mangiato alla cinese, all'indiana e pure all'italiana**
*fee-**goo**-ra-tee! **tcher**-a dee **toot**-to. ab-**ya**-mo man-**djat**-o **al**-la tchee-**nez**-ay, al-leen-**dyan**-a ay **poo**-ray al-leet-al-**ya**-na*
No it wasn't! You could get anything. We ate Chinese food, Indian food, and even Italian food!

Grusci **La pizza l'abbiamo trovata buona come da noi. Insomma tutta roba OK**
*la **peets**-tsa lab-**ya**-mo tro-**va**-ta **bwon**-a **kom**-ay da noy-ee. een-**som**-ma **toot**-ta **rob**-a o-**kay***
We found the pizza just as good as what you get at home. So everything was absolutely fine

Vito **La sera, poi, abbiamo visitato dei pub dove c'era sempre musica di ogni genere**
*la **ser**-a, pwoy, ab-**ya**-mo vee-zee-**tat**-o **day**-ee poob **dov**-ay **tchay**-ra **sem**-pray **moo**-zee-ka dee **on**-yee **djen**-er-ay*
And in the evenings we went to pubs where there was always music – all kinds of music

Grusci **Roba pop, funk, jazz. Tipi veramente in gamba**
***rob**-a pop, foonk, djats. **tee**-pee ver-a-**men**-tay een **gam**-ba*
Pop, funk, jazz. Really great bands

Dario **Beati voi! Vedo che vi siete proprio divertiti**
*bay-**at**-ee voy! **ved**-o kay vee **syet**-ay **prop**-ree-o dee-ver-**tee**-tee*
Lucky you! I can see you had a really great time

from the dialogue

non ci si vede
*non tchee see **ved**-ay*
we haven't seen each other

mi è piacuta molto(a)
*mee ay pyatch-**oo**-ta **molt**-o(a)*
I really liked it

cosa avete fatto di bello?
***ko**-za a-**vet**-ay **fat**-to dee **bel**-lo?*
did you do anything interesting?

uno schifo
***oo**-no **skee**-fo*
rubbish

c'era di tutto
***tcher**-a dee **toot**-to*
there were all sorts

come da noi
***kom**-ay da noy*
just like at home

di ogni genere
*dee **on**-yee **djen**-er-ay*
all different kinds

in gamba
*een **gam**-ba*
really good

beati voi!
*bay-**at**-ee voy!*
lucky you!

That London place

The style of language is different in this dialogue – Dario, Vito and his girlfriend Grusci speak an informal style of Italian with various colloquial expressions. You hear these used widely, and not just among younger people, so it is as well to recognise them at least. There aren't always informal equivalents in English. In quel di Londra means literally 'in that place called London'. It's a 'hip' way of describing somewhere and giving it familiarity. Figurati is a useful emphatic word which can be translated in a number of ways: 'don't mention it!', 'what are you saying?' or 'don't you believe it!'.

Inglese or italese?

Did you notice the mix of languages? – roba pop, funk, jazz 'pop, funk and jazz stuff'. It is a fairly common example of Italian and English coming together, the result of which is colloquially known as 'Italese'.

Past participles

Past participles end in -ato for regular -are verbs (mangiare – mangiato, visitare – visitato), in -uto for regular -ere verbs (vendere – venduto, credere – creduto) and -ito for regular -ire verbs (dormire – dormito, finire – finito). Some common verbs have irregular past participles, such as prendere – preso 'to get', dire – detto 'to say', vedere – visto 'to see', spendere – speso 'to spend'. If you are not sure of the past participle, you should look them up in a dictionary.

Just visiting

In Italian visitare means 'to go to' a city, a town or a place. So abbiamo visitato dei pub e dei club translates as 'we went to' places (pubs in this case!). If you go to see a person you just use the verb to go andare followed by da, as in siamo andati da Mario 'we went to pay a visit to Mario'.

To have or to be

Looking at the two examples: abbiamo mangiato 'we ate' and siamo stati 'we've been', the first takes avere for the perfect tense, and the second takes essere. A rough guide to this is that verbs that take an object, for example to eat (where you eat something) and to get (where you get something), take avere. Verbs that don't have an object, such as verbs of movement: venire 'to come', andare 'to go', arrivare 'to arrive', partire 'to leave', etc, take essere. It is also used to form the past of reflexive verbs: dove vi siete cacciati? 'where've you been hiding?', lui si è trasferito a Londra 'he moved to London'. You can find out from a dictionary whether a verb uses essere or avere to form the Italian perfect tense.

A complicated past?

When the perfect is formed with avere, then the past participle does not agree. Easy! Well, not quite .... If you throw into your sentence an object, and you put that object before the verb, then you need the agreement. So while you could easily say abbiamo trovato la pizza buona 'we found the pizza good', you could complicate things slightly by saying la pizza abbiamo trovata buona (where because la pizza has come before the verb, the feminine ending has to be given to the past participle). All this may seem a bit tricky until you get used to it. But pazienza! ('patience') as Italians exclaim when there's some difficulty that has to be put up with.

Men rule

Did you notice that Grusci said siamo stati ... 'we were at ...'? She has made stato – stati (plural) because two of them went, and if she had gone with her friend Carla, she would have said siamo state, (feminine plural). However, if you are talking about a mixed group (even 99 women and one man), then the agreeing past participle has to be masculine.

Agreeing with the past

When the verb essere is used to form the perfect tense, then the past participle behaves like an adjective – ie it has to agree with the subject. In the two examples where the subject is plural 'you', the past participle ends in -i (cacciati, diverti). In the sentence with the subject lui 'he', the past participle remains in the masculine singular (trasferito). If you are female, remember that when you are recounting where you have been, where you went, what time you arrived, etc, the past participle needs to be feminine: sono stata a Londra, sono andata a Buckingham Palace, sono arrivata alle sei, and so on.

did you know ...?

In Italian, people talk of making 'bridges' with their holidays by adding paid leave to bank holidays, which can occur in Italy in the middle of the week or a very long weekend. Thus abbiamo fatto un bel ponte (literally 'we have made a nice bridge') means that we took extra days in order to have a mini holiday.

now practise

> **past tenses**

extra vocabulary

great
fantastico(a)
*fan-**tas**-tee-ko(a)*

excellent
ottimo(a)
***ot**-tee-mo(a)*

it's disgusting
fa schifo
*fa **skee**-fo*

it's wonderful
è meraviglioso(a)
*ay mer-a-veel-**yo**-zo(a)*

how come?
come mai?
***ko**-may **ma**-ee?*

what a bore!
che barba!
*kay **bar**-ba!*

are you joking?
ma scherzi?
*ma **sker**-tsee?*

Word Zone (English–Italian)

A

a(n) un/una/uno

able: *to be able to* essere capace di

about su ; circa
a book about... un libro su...
about ten o'clock circa le dieci

above sopra

abroad all'estero *(m)*

to accept accettare

accident l'incidente *(m)*

address l'indirizzo *(m)*

adult l'adulto(a)
for adults per adulti

afraid: *to be afraid* avere paura

after dopo

afternoon il pomeriggio
this afternoon oggi pomeriggio
tomorrow afternoon domani pomeriggio
in the afternoon di pomeriggio

again ancora ; di nuovo

age l'età *(f)*

ago fa
a week ago una settimana fa

AIDS l'AIDS *(m)*

airport l'aeroporto *(m)*

all tutto(a)

allergic to allergico(a) a

to allow permettere

all right *(agreed)* va bene
are you all right? sta bene?

almost quasi

alone solo(a)

already già

also anche

always sempre

a.m. del mattino

America l'America *(f)*

American americano(a)

and e

angry arrabbiato(a)

anniversary l'anniversario *(m)*

announcement l'annuncio *(m)*

annual annuale

another un altro/un'altra

answer la risposta

to answer rispondere

apartment l'appartamento *(m)*

apple la mela

appointment l'appuntamento *(m)*

approximately circa

April aprile

architect *m/f* l'architetto

arm il braccio

arrivals *(plane, train)* gli arrivi

to arrive arrivare

art gallery la galleria d'arte ;
la pinacoteca

arthritis l'artrite *(f)*

artist *m/f* l'artista

to ask *(question)* domandare
(for something) chiedere

at a
at home a casa
at 8 o'clock alle otto
at once subito
at night di notte

August agosto

aunt la zia

Australia l'Australia *(f)*

Australian australiano(a)

autumn l'autunno *(m)*

available disponibile

average medio(a)

to avoid evitare

awful terribile

B

baby il/la bambino(a)

back *(of body)* la schiena

bad *(food)* andato(a) a male
(weather, news) brutto(a)

bag la borsa

baggage i bagagli

baker's la panetteria ; il panificio

bald *(person)* calvo(a)
(tyre) liscio(a)

ball *(large)* il pallone
(small) la pallina

balloon il palloncino

bank la banca

bank account il conto in banca

bar il bar

basement il seminterrato

bath il bagno
to have a bath fare un bagno

bathroom il bagno

battery *(radio, etc)* la pila
(car) la batteria

to be essere

beach la spiaggia

beard la barba

beautiful bello(a)

because perché

to become diventare

bed il letto

bedroom la camera da letto

beer la birra

before prima di

to begin cominciare

behind dietro di

to believe credere

bell *(church)* la campana
(doorbell) il campanello

to belong to appartenere a

below sotto

beside *(next to)* accanto a
beside the bank accanto alla banca

best: *the best* il/la migliore

better (than) meglio (di)

between fra

bicycle la bicicletta ; la bici
by bicycle in bicicletta

big grande
bigger (than) più grande (di)

bill *(hotel, restaurant)* il conto
(for work done) la fattura
(gas, telephone) la bolletta

birth la nascita

birthday il compleanno
happy birthday! buon compleanno
my birthday is on... il mio compleanno è il...

bit il pezzo
a bit un po'

to bite *(animal)* mordere
(insect) morsicare

black nero(a)

blind *(person)* cieco(a)

blond *(person)* biondo(a)

blood il sangue

blouse la camicetta

blue *(light)* azzurro(a)
dark blue blu scuro
light blue azzurro(a)

boat la barca ; il battello

body il corpo

book il libro

to book prenotare

booking la prenotazione

boring noioso(a)

born: *to be born* essere nato(a)

to borrow prendere in prestito

both tutti e due

bottle la bottiglia

box la scatola

boy *(young child)* il bambino
(teenage) il ragazzo

boyfriend il ragazzo

bread il pane

to break rompere

breakfast la (prima) colazione

bridge il ponte

to bring portare

Britain la Gran Bretagna

British britannico(a)

broken rotto(a)

brother il fratello

brother-in-law il cognato

brown marrone

brush la spazzola

to build costruire

to burn bruciare
(CD) masterizzare

bus l'autobus *(m)*

bus station la stazione delle autolinee

bus stop la fermata (dell'autobus)

business gli affari

busy occupato(a) ; impegnato(a)

but ma ; però

butcher's il macellaio

butter il burro

to buy comprare

by *(next to)* accanto a
(via) via
by bus in autobus
by car in macchina
by train in treno
by ship in battello

C

café il bar

cake *(big)* la torta
(small) il pasticcino

to call chiamare
(phone) chiamare per telefono

camera la macchina fotografica

to camp campeggiare

campsite il campeggio

can il barattolo ; la scatola

can *(to be able)* potere

can opener l'apriscatole *(m)*

Canada il Canada

Canadian canadese

to cancel cancellare ; annullare

cancellation la cancellazione

capital *(city)* la capitale

car la macchina ; l'auto *(m)*

car hire l'autonoleggio *(m)*

car park il parcheggio

caravan la roulotte

card *(greetings)* il biglietto d'auguri
(business) il biglietto da visita
(playing cards) le carte da gioco

careful attento(a)
to be careful fare attenzione

carriage *(railway)* il vagone

to carry portare

case *(suitcase)* la valigia

to cash *(cheque)* incassare

cash desk la cassa

castle il castello

cat il gatto

to catch *(train, etc)* prendere

cathedral il duomo

CD il CD

CD player il lettore CD

cellar la cantina

centre il centro

chair la sedia

change il cambio
(money returned) il resto

to change: *to change money* cambiare soldi
to change clothes cambiarsi
to change train cambiare treno

Channel *(English)* la Manica

charge *(fee)* la tariffa

cheap economico(a)

to check controllare

cheers! salute! ; cin-cin!

cheese il formaggio

chemist's la farmacia

cheque l'assegno *(m)*

chicken il pollo

child il/la bambino(a)

children *(small)* i bambini
(older children) i ragazzi

chips *(french fries)* le patatine fritte

chocolate la cioccolata

to choose scegliere

Christian name il nome di battesimo

Christmas il Natale
Merry Christmas! Buon Natale!

Christmas Eve la vigilia di Natale

church la chiesa

cigarette la sigaretta

cigarette lighter l'accendino

cinema il cinema

city la città

city centre il centro città

clean pulito(a)

to clean pulire

clear chiaro(a)

client il/la cliente

clock l'orologio *(m)*

to close chiudere

closed *(shop, etc)* chiuso(a)

clothes i vestiti

coach il pullman

coat il cappotto

code il codice

coffee *(espresso)* il caffè
cappuccino il cappuccino

cold freddo(a)
I'm cold ho freddo
it's cold fa freddo

cold *(illness)* il raffreddore

to collect raccogliere
(to collect someone) andare a prendere

colour il colore

comb il pettine

to come venire
(to arrive) arrivare
to come back tornare

company *(firm)* la ditta

to complain fare un reclamo

to complete *(finish)* finire
(form) riempire

compulsory obbligatorio(a)

computer il computer

computer game il videogioco

concert il concerto

concession la riduzione

conference il congresso

to confirm confermare

confirmation la conferma

to continue continuare

to cook cucinare

cooker la cucina

cool fresco(a)

copy la copia

to copy copiare

corkscrew il cavatappi

corner l'angolo *(m)*

corridor il corridoio

to cost costare
how much does it cost? quanto costa?

cough la tosse

country *(not town)* la campagna
(nation) il paese

couple *(two people)* la coppia
a couple of... un paio di...

course *(of meal)* il piatto

cousin il/la cugino(a)

cream *(lotion)* la crema
(dairy) la panna

credit card la carta di credito

crisps le patatine

to cross *(road)* attraversare

crossroads l'incrocio *(m)*

crowd la folla

cruise la crociera

to cry *(weep)* piangere

cup la tazza

cupboard l'armadio *(m)*

custom *(tradition)* il costume

customer il/la cliente

customs *(duty)* la dogana

to cut tagliare

to cycle andare in bicicletta

D

daily *(each day)* ogni giorno ; quotidiano(a)

to dance ballare

dangerous pericoloso(a)

dark *(colour)* scuro(a)
(night) buio(a)

date la data

date of birth la data di nascita

daughter la figlia

daughter-in-law la nuora

day il giorno
per day al giorno
every day ogni giorno
(span of time) la giornata

dead morto(a)

deaf sordo(a)

dear caro(a)

December dicembre

deep profondo(a)

delay il ritardo

delicious delizioso(a)

dentist il/la dentista

to depart partire

department il reparto

department store il grande magazzino

departure la partenza

to describe descrivere

desk la scrivania
(information, etc) il banco

dessert il dolce

detour la deviazione

to develop *(photos)* sviluppare

to dial fare il numero

dialling code il prefisso telefonico

diary l'agenda *(f)*

dictionary il dizionario

to die morire

diesel il gasolio

diet la dieta
I'm on a diet sono a dieta

difficult difficile

digital camera la fotocamera digitale

dining room la sala da pranzo

dinner *(evening meal)* la cena
to have dinner cenare

directions le indicazioni
to ask for directions chiedere la strada

directory *(telephone)* l'elenco telefonico *(m)*

dirty sporco(a)

disabled *(person)* disabile ; handicappato(a)

to disagree non essere d'accordo

to disappear scomparire

to discover scoprire

to disturb disturbare

divorced divorziato(a)

to do fare

doctor il medico/la dottoressa

documents i documenti

dog il cane

door la porta

doorbell il campanello

down: *to go down* scendere

downstairs giù ; dabbasso

dress il vestito

to dress *(oneself)* vestirsi

to drink bere

drinking water l'acqua potabile *(f)*

to drive guidare

driver *(of car)* l'autista *(m/f)*

drug *(medicine)* il farmaco
(narcotics) la droga

drunk ubriaco(a)

dry secco(a) ; asciutto(a)

to dry asciugare

during durante

E

each ogni

ear l'orecchio *(m)*

early presto

to earn guadagnare

earphones le cuffie

earrings gli orecchini

earth la terra

east l'est *(m)*

Easter la Pasqua

easy facile

to eat mangiare

egg l'uovo *(m)*
eggs le uova

either ... or o ... o

elevator l'ascensore *(m)*

e-mail l'e-mail *(f)*
to e-mail s.o. mandare un'e-mail a qualcuno

e-mail address l'indirizzo di posta elettronica *(m)*

emergency l'emergenza *(f)*

empty vuoto(a)

end la fine

engaged *(to be married)* fidanzato(a)
(phone, toilet, etc) occupato(a)

engine il motore

England l'Inghilterra *(f)*

English inglese
(language) l'inglese *(m)*

to enjoy divertirsi
(to like) piacere
I enjoyed the trip la gita mi è piaciuta
I enjoy swimming mi piace nuotare
enjoy your meal! buon appetito!

enough abbastanza

to enter entrare

entrance l'entrata *(f)* ; l'ingresso *(m)*

error l'errore *(m)*

to escape fuggire

euro l'euro *(m)*

Europe l'Europa *(f)*

European europeo(a)

European Union l'Unione Europea *(f)*

evening la sera
this evening stasera
tomorrow evening domani sera

every ogni ; ciascuno ; tutti

everyone tutti

everything tutto

everywhere dappertutto

examination l'esame *(m)*

example: *for example* per esempio

excellent ottimo(a)

to exchange cambiare

exchange rate il cambio

exciting emozionante

excursion l'escursione *(f)*

excuse me! *(sorry)* mi scusi!
(when passing) permesso!

exhibition la mostra

exit l'uscita *(f)*

expenses le spese

expensive costoso(a) ; caro(a)

to expire *(ticket, etc)* scadere

to explain spiegare

extra *(spare)* in più
(more) supplementare

eye l'occhio *(m)*

F

face la faccia

fair *(just)* giusto(a)
(blond) biondo(a)

fair *(trade)* la fiera
(funfair) il luna park

fall *(autumn)* l'autunno *(m)*

to fall cadere

family la famiglia

famous famoso(a)

fan *(hand-held)* il ventaglio
(electric) il ventilatore
(football) il/la tifoso(a)

far lontano(a)

fare la tariffa

fast veloce
too fast troppo veloce

fat grasso(a)
(noun) il grasso

father il padre

father-in-law il suocero

fault *(defect)* il difetto
it's not my fault non è colpa mia

favourite preferito(a)

fax il fax
by fax per fax

to fax mandare un fax

February febbraio

to feed dare da mangiare

to feel sentire ; sentirsi
I don't feel well non mi sento bene

feet i piedi

female femmina ; femminile

festival la festa

to fetch *(bring)* portare
(to go and get) andare a prendere

fever la febbre

few pochi
a few alcuni

fiancé(e) il/la fidanzato(a)

to fight combattere ; lottare

to fill riempire

fill it up! *(petrol)* il pieno!

film *(at cinema)* il film
(for camera) la pellicola

to find trovare

fine *(to be paid)* la multa

finger il dito

to finish finire

fire il fuoco ; l'incendio *(m)*

fire brigade i vigili del fuoco

firm *(company)* l'azienda *(f)* ; la ditta

first primo(a)

first aid il pronto soccorso

first name il nome di battesimo

fish il pesce

to fish pescare

fishmonger's la pescheria

to fit *(clothes)* andare bene

to fix riparare ; sistemare

fizzy gassato(a)

flag la bandiera

flat l'appartamento *(m)*

flat piatto(a)
flat battery la batteria scarica
flat tyre la gomma a terra

flavour il gusto

flight il volo

flood l'alluvione *(f)*

floor *(of building)* il piano
(of room) il pavimento
on the ground floor al pianterreno
on the first floor al primo piano

flower i fiori

fly la mosca

to fly volare

fog la nebbia

to follow seguire

foot il piede
on foot a piedi

football il calcio ; il pallone

for per
for me/us per me/noi

forbidden proibito(a)

foreign straniero(a)

forever per sempre

to forget dimenticare

fork *(for eating)* la forchetta
(in road) il bivio

form *(document)* il modulo

forward avanti

France la Francia

free *(not occupied)* libero(a)
(costing nothing) gratis

French francese
(language) il francese

fresh fresco(a)

Friday il venerdì

fridge il frigorifero

fried fritto(a)

friend l'amico(a)

from da
from Scotland dalla Scozia
from England dall'Inghilterra

front davanti
in front of... di fronte a...

fruit la frutta

full pieno(a)
(occupied) completo(a)

fun il divertimento

funny *(amusing)* divertente

furniture i mobili

G

game il gioco

garage *(private)* il garage
(for repairs) l'autofficina *(f)*
(for petrol) la stazione di servizio

garden il giardino

gear *(car)* la marcia
neutral folle
reverse la retromarcia

gents' *(toilet)* la toilette (per uomini)

genuine *(leather, silver)* vero(a)
(antique, etc) autentico(a)

German tedesco(a)
(language) il tedesco

Germany la Germania

to get *(obtain)* ottenere
(to receive) ricevere
(to fetch) prendere

to get in/on *(vehicle)* salire in/su

to get off *(bus, etc)* scendere da

gift il regalo

girl *(young child)* la bambina
(teenage) la ragazza

girlfriend la ragazza

to give dare

to give back restituire

glass *(substance)* il vetro
(for drinking) il bicchiere

glasses *(specs)* gli occhiali

to go andare

to go back ritornare

to go in entrare in

to go out *(leave)* uscire

gold l'oro *(m)*

good buono(a)
(pleasant) bello(a)

goodbye arrivederci

good day buon giorno

good evening buona sera

good night buona notte

grandchild il/la nipote

granddaughter la nipotina

grandfather il nonno

grandmother la nonna

grandparents i nonni

grandson il nipotino

great *(big)* grande
(wonderful) fantastico(a)

Great Britain la Gran Bretagna

green verde

grocer's il negozio di alimentari

ground la terra

ground floor il pianterreno

guesthouse la pensione

guide *(tourist)* la guida

guidebook la guida

guided tour la visita guidata

H

hair i capelli

half la metà
half an hour mezz'ora

half-price metà prezzo

ham *(cooked)* il prosciutto cotto
(cured) il prosciutto crudo

hand la mano

handbag la borsa

handkerchief il fazzoletto

handsome bello(a)

to happen succedere
what happened? cos'è successo?

happy felice
happy birthday! buon compleanno!

harbour il porto

hard duro(a)
(difficult) difficile

hat il cappello

to have avere

to have to dovere

head la testa

headache il mal di testa

headphones la cuffia

health la salute

healthy sano(a)

to hear sentire

heart il cuore

heart attack l'infarto *(m)*

heating il riscaldamento

heavy pesante

height l'altezza *(f)*

hello! salve! ; ciao!
(on telephone) pronto

helmet il casco

to help aiutare
can you help me? può aiutarmi?

her il/la suo(a)

here qui
here is... ecco...

to hide nascondere

high alto(a)
(speed) forte

hill la collina

him lui ; lo ; gli

hire il noleggio

to hire noleggiare

his il/la suo(a)

to hit colpire

hobby il passatempo

to hold tenere
(to contain) contenere

hole il buco

holiday la festa
on holiday in vacanza

home la casa
at home a casa

honeymoon la luna di miele

to hope sperare
I hope so/not spero di sì/no

horse il cavallo

to horse-ride andare a cavallo

hospital l'ospedale *(m)*

hot caldo(a)
I'm hot ho caldo
it's hot (weather) fa caldo

hotel l'albergo *(m)* ; l'hotel *(m)*

hour l'ora *(f)*

house la casa

housewife la casalinga

how? *(in what way)* come?
how much? quanto(a)?
how many? quanti(e)?

hungry: *to be hungry* avere fame

hurry: *I'm in a hurry* ho fretta

to hurt fare male
that hurts fa male

husband il marito

hydrofoil l'aliscafo *(m)*

I

ice il ghiaccio

ice cream il gelato

identity card la carta d'identità

if se

ill malato(a)

immediately subito

important importante

impossible impossibile

to improve migliorare

in in
in 2 hours in due ore
in London a Londra

in front of davanti a

included compreso(a) ; incluso(a)

to increase aumentare

indoors dentro ; al chiuso

information le informazioni

inside dentro

instead of invece di

insurance l'assicurazione *(f)*

to intend to avere intenzione di

interesting interessante

internet l'Internet *(m)*

internet café il cyber-café

interval l'intervallo *(m)*

interview l'intervista *(f)*

into in
into town in città

to introduce someone to presentare qualcuno a

invitation l'invito *(m)*

to invite invitare

Ireland l'Irlanda *(f)*

Irish irlandese

iron *(for clothes)* il ferro da stiro
(metal) il ferro

is è

island l'isola *(f)*

Italian italiano(a)
(language) l'italiano *(m)*

Italy l'Italia *(f)*

J

jacket la giacca

jam *(food)* la marmellata

January gennaio

jeans i blue jeans

job il lavoro

to join *(club)* iscriversi a

to join in *(game)* partecipare a

to joke scherzare

journey il viaggio

juice il succo
orange juice il succo d'arancia

July luglio

June giugno

just: *just two* solamente due
I've just arrived sono appena arrivato(a)

K

to keep *(retain)* tenere

key la chiave

kilo il chilo
2 kilos due chili

kilogram il chilogrammo

kind *(person)* gentile

kind *(sort)* il tipo

to kiss baciare

kitchen la cucina

knee il ginocchio

knife il coltello

to knock *(on door)* bussare

to knock down *(in car)* investire

to knock over *(glass, vase)* rovesciare

to know sapere
(to be acquainted with) conoscere

L

lady la signora

lake il lago

land la terra

language la lingua

large grande

last ultimo(a) ; scorso(a)
the last bus l'ultimo autobus
last night ieri notte
last week la settimana scorsa
last time l'ultima volta

late tardi
the train's late il treno è in ritardo

later più tardi

to laugh ridere

lavatory la toilette

to learn imparare

leather il cuoio ; la pelle

to leave *(leave behind)* lasciare
(train, bus, etc) partire

left la sinistra
on/to the left a sinistra

leg la gamba

lemon il limone

to lend prestare

length la lunghezza

lens *(camera)* l'obiettivo *(m)*
(contact lens) la lente a contatto

less meno
less than meno di

to let *(allow)* permettere
(to hire out) affittare

letter la lettera

library la biblioteca

licence il permesso
(driving) la patente

to lie down sdraiarsi

lift *(elevator)* l'ascensore *(m)*
(in car) il passaggio

light *(not heavy)* leggero(a)
(colour) chiaro(a)

light la luce

like come

to like piacere
I like coffee mi piace il caffè
I don't like... non mi piace...

lips le labbra

list l'elenco *(m)* ; la lista

to listen (to) ascoltare

litre il litro

little *(small)* piccolino(a)
a little... un po' di...

to live vivere ; abitare
I live in London vivo a Londra
he lives in a flat abita in un appartamento

living room il salotto

to lock chiudere a chiave

London Londra
in/to London a Londra

long lungo(a)
for a long time molto tempo

to look at guardare

to look for cercare

lorry il camion

to lose perdere

lost *(object)* perso(a)
I've lost my... ho perso il/la...
I'm lost mi sono smarrito(a)

lot: *a lot* molto

lottery la lotteria

loud forte

lounge *(in hotel)* il salone
(in house) la sala

love l'amore *(m)*

to love *(person)* amare
I love you ti amo
I love swimming mi piace nuotare

lovely bellissimo(a)

low basso(a)

luggage i bagagli

lunch il pranzo

M

mad *(insane)* matto(a)
(angry) arrabbiato(a)

magazine la rivista

maiden name il nome da ragazza

mail la posta

main principale

main course *(meal)* il secondo

to make *(generally)* fare
(meal) preparare

male maschio ; maschile

man l'uomo *(m)*

to manage *(be in charge of)* dirigere

manager il direttore ; il gerente

many molti(e)

map la mappa

March marzo

market il mercato

married sposato(a)

match *(game)* la partita

matches i fiammiferi

to matter importare
it doesn't matter non importa
what's the matter? cosa c'è?

May maggio

me me ; mi

meal il pasto

to mean *(signify)* voler dire
what does it mean? cosa vuol dire?

meat la carne

to meet incontrare
pleased to meet you! piacere!

meeting la riunione
(by chance) l'incontro *(m)*

member *(of club, etc)* il/la socio(a)

memory la memoria
(memories) i ricordi

men gli uomini

to mend riparare

menu il menù
set menu il menù a prezzo fisso
à la carte menu il menù alla carta

message il messaggio

metre il metro

midday il mezzogiorno
at midday a mezzogiorno

midnight la mezzanotte
at midnight a mezzanotte

milk il latte

mind: *do you mind?* le dà fastidio?
I don't mind non mi dà fastidio

mineral water l'acqua minerale *(f)*

minute il minuto

mirror lo specchio

to miss *(train, etc)* perdere

Miss Signorina

mistake l'errore *(m)*

mobile phone il cellulare

Monday il lunedì

money i soldi

month il mese

moon la luna

more (than) più (di)
more than 3 più di tre
more wine ancora un po' di vino

morning la mattina
in the morning di mattina
this morning stamattina
tomorrow morning domani mattina

most il/la più ; il massimo

mother la madre

mother-in-law la suocera

motor il motore

motorbike la moto

motorway l'autostrada *(f)*

mountain la montagna

mountain bike la mountain bike

mouse il topo
(computer) il mouse

mouth la bocca

move muoversi

Mr Signor

Mrs Signora

Ms Signora

much molto
too much troppo

museum il museo

music la musica

must *(to have to)* dovere

my il/la mio(a)

N

nail *(metal)* il chiodo
(fingernail) l'unghia *(f)*

name il nome
my name is... mi chiamo...

nappies i pannolini

narrow stretto(a)

nationality la nazionalità

natural naturale

navy blue blu marino

near to vicino(a) a

necessary necessario(a)

neck il collo

to need avere bisogno di...

neighbour il/la vicino(a)

nephew il nipote

net la rete
the Net l'Internet *(m)*

never mai

new nuovo(a)

news le notizie
(on television) il telegiornale

newsagent's il giornalaio

newspaper il giornale

New Year il Capodanno
happy New Year! buon Anno!

New Year's Eve la notte di San Silvestro ; l'ultimo dell'anno *(m)*

New Zealand la Nuova Zelanda

next prossimo(a)
next to accanto(a) a
next week la settimana prossima
the next bus il prossimo autobus

nice piacevole
(person) simpatico(a)

niece la nipote

night la notte
at night di notte

nightdress la camicia da notte

no no
no entry vietato l'ingresso
no smoking vietato fumare

nobody nessuno

noise il rumore

none nessuno(a)

non-smoking per non-fumatori

north il nord

Northern Ireland l'Irlanda del Nord *(f)*

nose il naso

not non

nothing niente
nothing else nient'altro

notice l'avviso *(m)*

November novembre

now adesso

nowhere da nessuna parte

number il numero

nurse l'infermiera(e) *(f/m)*

nut *(to eat)* la noce
(for bolt) il dado

O

to obtain ottenere

October ottobre

odd *(strange)* strano(a)

of di
made of... fatto di...

off *(machine, etc)* spento(a)
(milk, food) andato(a) a male

office l'ufficio *(m)*

often spesso
how often? ogni quanto?

oil l'olio *(m)*

OK! va bene!

old vecchio(a)
I'm ... years old ho ... anni

on *(light, engine)* acceso(a)
(tap) aperto(a)
on the table sulla tavola
on time in orario

once una volta
at once subito

only solo(a)

open aperto(a)

to open aprire

opposite di fronte a

or o

orange *(colour)* arancione

orange *(fruit)* l'arancia *(f)*

orange juice il succo d'arancia

to order *(food, etc)* ordinare

to organize organizzare

other l'altro(a)

our il/la nostro(a)

out *(light)* spento(a)
he/she's out è fuori
he's gone out è uscito

outdoor *(pool, etc)* all'aperto

outside: *it's outside* è fuori

oven il forno

over *(on top of)* sopra

to overtake sorpassare

to owe dovere

owner il/la proprietario(a)

P

to pack *(suitcase)* fare la valigia

packet il pacchetto

page la pagina

paid pagato(a)

painful doloroso(a)

painkiller l'analgesico *(m)*

to paint *(wall, etc)* verniciare
(picture) dipingere

panties le mutandine

pants le mutande

paper la carta

parents i genitori

park il parco

to park parcheggiare

partner *(business)* il/la socio(a)
(boy/girlfriend) il/la compagno(a)

party *(celebration)* la festa
(political) il partito

pass *(mountain)* il valico
(bus, train) la tessera

passenger il/la passeggero(a)

passport il passaporto

path il sentiero

to pay pagare

payment il pagamento

peaches le pesche

pears le pere

pen la penna

pencil la matita

pensioner il/la pensionato(a)

people la gente

per per ; a
per day al giorno
per week alla settimana
100 km per hour 100 km all'ora

perfect perfetto(a)

perfume il profumo

perhaps forse

permit il permesso

person la persona

pet l'animale domestico *(m)*

petrol la benzina
unleaded petrol la benzina senza piombo

petrol station la stazione di servizio

pharmacy la farmacia

phone il telefono
by phone per telefono

to phone telefonare

phonebook l'elenco telefonico *(m)*

phonebox la cabina telefonica

photograph la foto
to take a photo fare una foto

to pick *(fruit, flowers)* cogliere
(to choose) scegliere

picnic il picnic
to have a picnic fare un picnic

picture *(painting)* il quadro
(photo) la foto

piece il pezzo

pill la pillola
to be on the pill prendere la pillola

pink rosa

pity: *what a pity!* che peccato!

place il luogo

place of birth il luogo di nascita

plain *(obvious)* chiaro(a)
(unflavoured) naturale

plan il piano

plane l'aereo *(m)*

plate il piatto

platform *(railway)* il binario

to play *(games)* giocare

please per favore

pleased: *pleased to meet you* piacere

p.m. del pomeriggio

pocket la tasca

poison il veleno

police la polizia

policeman il poliziotto

pool *(swimming)* la piscina

poor povero(a)

port *(seaport, wine)* il porto

post: *by post* per posta

postbox la buca delle lettere

postcard la cartolina

post office la posta

to postpone rimandare

potato la patata

pound *(money)* la sterlina

to pour versare

powder: *in powder form* in polvere

to prefer preferire

to prepare preparare

present *(gift)* il regalo

pretty carino(a)

price il prezzo

print *(photo)* la foto

private privato(a)

prize il premio

problem il problema

programme il programma

prohibited proibito(a)

to promise promettere

to provide fornire

public pubblico(a)

public holiday la festa nazionale

pudding il dessert

to pull tirare

puncture la gomma a terra

purple viola

purse il borsellino

to push spingere

to put *(to place)* mettere

pyjamas il pigiama

Q

quality la qualità

quantity la quantità

to quarrel litigare

queen la regina

question la domanda

to queue fare la coda

quick veloce

quiet *(place)* tranquillo(a)

quite *(rather)* abbastanza

R

race *(sport)* la gara

radio la radio

railway station la stazione dei treni

rain la pioggia

to rain piovere

raincoat l'impermeabile *(m)*

rare *(unique)* raro(a)
(steak) al sangue

rate *(cost)* la tariffa

razor il rasoio

to read leggere

ready pronto(a)
to get ready prepararsi

real vero(a)

receipt la ricevuta

reception *(desk)* la reception

receptionist l'addetto(a)

to recognize riconoscere

to recommend raccomandare

red rosso(a)

to reduce ridurre

reduction la riduzione

to refuse rifiutare

regarding riguardo a

region la regione

relationship il rapporto

to remain restare ; rimanere

to remember ricordare
I don't remember non mi ricordo

to remove togliere

rent l'affitto *(m)*

to rent *(house)* affittare
(car) noleggiare

rental *(house)* l'affitto *(m)*
(car) il nolo

to repair riparare

to repeat ripetere

to reply rispondere

reservation la prenotazione

to reserve prenotare

rest *(repose)* il riposo
(remainder) il resto

to rest riposarsi

restaurant il ristorante

retired: ***I'm retired*** sono in pensione

to return *(go back)* ritornare
(to give back) restituire

return ticket il biglietto di andata e ritorno

reverse gear la retromarcia

rice il riso

rich ricco(a)

to ride a horse andare a cavallo

right *(correct)* giusto(a)

right la destra
at/to the right a destra
on the right sulla destra

to ring *(bell)* suonare
(phone) squillare

ring l'anello *(m)*

river il fiume

road la strada

roast arrosto(a)

roof il tetto

room *(hotel)* la camera
(space) lo spazio

rose la rosa

round rotondo(a)

rubbish la spazzatura

rucksack lo zaino

to run correre

S

sad triste

safe *(for valuables)* la cassaforte

safe *(medicine, etc)* senza pericolo ; sicuro(a)

salary lo stipendio

salt il sale

same stesso(a)

sand la sabbia

sandals i sandali

sandwich il panino ; il tramezzino
toasted sandwich il toast

Saturday il sabato

sauce la salsa

to save *(life)* salvare
(money) risparmiare

to say dire

scarf la sciarpa
(headscarf) il foulard

school la scuola
primary school la scuola elementare
secondary school il liceo

scissors le forbici

Scotland la Scozia

Scottish scozzese

screen lo schermo

screwdriver il cacciavite

sea il mare

seaside: ***at the seaside*** al mare

season *(of year)* la stagione
in season di stagione

seat *(chair)* la sedia
(theatre, plane, etc) il posto

seatbelt la cintura di sicurezza

second *(time)* il secondo

second secondo(a)

second-hand di seconda mano

secretary la segretaria

to see vedere

to sell vendere

to send mandare ; spedire ; inviare

senior citizen l'anziano(a)

separated separato(a)

September settembre

serious grave
(not funny) serio(a)

to serve servire

service station la stazione di servizio

set menu il menù turistico

settee il divano

several alcuni(e)

to share dividere

to shave farsi la barba

shirt la camicia

shoe la scarpa

shop il negozio

to shop fare la spesa

shop assistant il/la commesso(a)

shopping centre il centro commerciale

short corto(a)
(person) basso(a)

to shout gridare

to show mostrare

shower la doccia
(rain) il rovescio
to take a shower fare la doccia

shut *(closed)* chiuso(a)

sick *(ill)* malato(a)
(nauseous) nauseato(a)

side il lato

sign il segno
(on road) il segnale

to sign firmare

signature la firma

silk la seta

silver l'argento *(m)*

similar to simile a

since *(time)* da

to sing cantare

single *(unmarried)* non sposato(a)
(not double) singolo(a)
(ticket) di (sola) andata

sister la sorella

sister-in-law la cognata

to sit sedersi

size *(of clothes)* la taglia
(of shoes) il numero

to ski sciare

skin la pelle

skirt la gonna

sky il cielo

to sleep dormire

slice *(piece of)* la fetta

to slip scivolare

slow lento(a)

to slow down rallentare

small piccolo(a)
smaller (than) più piccolo (di)

smell l'odore (m)
bad smell il puzzo
nice smell il profumo
to smile sorridere
to smoke fumare
smooth liscio(a)
snack lo spuntino
to have a snack fare lo spuntino
snow la neve
to snow: *it's snowing* nevica
soap il sapone
socks i calzini
soft soffice ; morbido(a)
some di (del/della)
(a few) alcuni/alcune
someone qualcuno
something qualcosa
sometimes qualche volta
son il figlio
son-in-law il genero
soon presto
as soon as possible il più presto possibile
sore throat il mal di gola
sorry: *I'm sorry!* mi scusi!
sort il tipo
what sort? che tipo?
south il sud
Spain la Spagna
Spanish spagnolo(a)
sparkling frizzante
to speak parlare
do you speak English? parla inglese?
special speciale
to spell scrivere
how's it spelt? come si scrive?
to spend spendere
to spill rovesciare
spoon il cucchiaio
spring *(season)* la primavera
(metal) la molla
square *(in town)* la piazza
stairs le scale
stamp il francobollo
to stand stare in piedi
star la stella
to start cominciare
starter *(food)* l'antipasto *(m)*
(in car) il motorino d'avviamento
station la stazione
stay il soggiorno
to stay *(remain)* rimanere
I'm staying at the Grand Hotel sono al Grand Hotel
to steal rubare
stepdaughter la figliastra
stepfather il patrigno
stepmother la matrigna
stepson il figliastro
still *(motionless)* fermo(a)
(water) naturale
(yet) ancora
stolen rubato(a)
stomach lo stomaco ; la pancia
stomachache il mal di pancia
to stop *(come to a halt)* fermarsi
(stop doing something) smettere
store *(shop)* il negozio
storey il piano
storm la tempesta ; il temporale
story il racconto
straightaway subito
straight on diritto
straw *(drinking)* la cannuccia
strawberries le fragole
street la strada
street map la piantina
strong forte
student lo studente/la studentessa
stupid stupido(a)
subtitles i sottotitoli
suddenly all'improvviso
sugar lo zucchero
suit *(man's)* l'abito *(m)*
(woman's) il tailleur
suitcase la valigia
summer l'estate *(f)*
sun il sole
Sunday la domenica
sunny: *it's sunny* c'è il sole
sunset il tramonto
sunstroke l'insolazione *(f)*
supermarket il supermercato
supplement il supplemento
to supply fornire
to surf fare il surf
to surf the net navigare in internet
surname il cognome
surprise la sorpresa
to swallow inghiottire
to sweat sudare
sweet *(not savoury)* dolce
sweets le caramelle
to swim nuotare
swimming pool la piscina
swimsuit il costume da bagno
Swiss svizzero(a)
switch l'interruttore *(m)*
to switch off spegnere
to switch on accendere
Switzerland la Svizzera

T

table la tavola
tablet *(pill)* la pastiglia
to take *(carry)* portare
(to grab, seize) prendere
how long does it take? quanto tempo ci vuole?
to talk parlare
tall alto(a)
tank *(car)* il serbatoio
tap il rubinetto
to taste assaggiare ; provare
taxi il taxi
tea il tè
herbal tea la tisana
tea pot la teiera
to teach insegnare

teacher l'insegnante *(m/f)*
team la squadra
teeth i denti
telephone il telefono
to telephone telefonare
telephone box la cabina telefonica
television la televisione
to tell dire
temperature la temperatura
to have a temperature avere la febbre
temporary provvisorio(a)
tenant l'inquilino(a)
tent la tenda
terrace la terrazza
to test *(try out)* provare
to thank ringraziare
thank you grazie
that quel/quella/quello
that one quello là
theatre il teatro
theft il furto
these questi(e)
thick spesso(a)
thin sottile
(person) magro(a)
thing la cosa
to think pensare
thirsty: *to be thirsty* avere sete
this questo(a)
those quei/quelle/quegli
throat la gola
through attraverso
thumb il pollice
thunderstorm il temporale
Thursday il giovedì
ticket *(bus, train, etc)* il biglietto
(entry fee) il biglietto d'ingresso
a single ticket un biglietto di (sola) andata
a return ticket un biglietto di andata e ritorno
tie la cravatta
tight stretto(a)
tights i collant ; la calzamaglia
till *(until)* fino a
time il tempo
(of day) l'ora *(f)*
this time questa volta
what time is it? che ore sono?
timetable l'orario *(m)*
tin *(can)* la scatola ; la lattina
tip *(to waiter, etc)* la mancia
tired stanco(a)
to a
to London a Londra
to the airport all'aeroporto
tobacconist's il tabaccaio
today oggi
together insieme
toilet la toilette
tomato il pomodoro
tomorrow domani
tomorrow morning domani mattina
tongue la lingua
tonight stasera
too *(also)* anche
too big troppo grande
too small troppo piccolo(a)
tooth il dente
toothbrush lo spazzolino da denti
toothpaste il dentifricio
top: *the top floor* l'ultimo piano *(m)*
torch *(flashlight)* la pila
tour guide la guida turistica
tourist il/la turista
tourist information le informazioni turistiche
towel l'asciugamano *(m)*
tower la torre
town la città
town centre il centro città
toy il giocattolo
traditional tradizionale
traffic il traffico
traffic jam l'ingorgo *(m)*
traffic lights il semaforo
train il treno
trainers le scarpe da ginnastica
to translate tradurre
to travel viaggiare
travel agent's l'agenzia di viaggi *(f)*
tree l'albero *(m)*
trip la gita ; il viaggio
trolley il carrello
trouble i problemi
truck il camion
true vero(a)
to try provare
Tuesday il martedì
tunnel la galleria
to turn *(handle, wheel)* girare
to turn around girarsi
to turn off *(light, etc)* spegnere
(tap) chiudere
to turn on *(light, etc)* accendere
(tap) aprire
twice due volte ; il doppio
tyre la gomma ; il pneumatico

U

ugly brutto(a)
umbrella l'ombrello *(m)*
(sunshade) l'ombrellone *(m)*
uncle lo zio
uncomfortable scomodo(a)
under sotto
underground *(metro)* la metropolitana
underpants le mutande
to understand capire
underwear la biancheria intima
to undress spogliarsi
United Kingdom il Regno Unito
United States gli Stati Uniti
university l'università *(f)*
to unlock aprire
to unplug staccare
to unscrew svitare
up: *to get up* alzarsi

upstairs di sopra
to use usare
useful utile
usually di solito

V

vacancy *(in hotel)* la camera libera
vacant libero(a)
vacation la vacanza
vase il vaso
VAT l'IVA *(f)*
vegan vegetaliano(a)
vegetables le verdure
vegetarian vegetariano(a)
vehicle il veicolo
very molto
vet il/la veterinario(a)
to video *(from TV)* registrare su videocassetta
to visit visitare
visitor il visitatore/la visitatrice

W

to wait (for) aspettare
waiter/waitress il cameriere/la cameriera
to wake up
(someone) svegliare
(oneself) svegliarsi
Wales il Galles
walk la passeggiata
to walk andare a piedi
wall il muro ; la parete
wallet il portafoglio
to want volere
war la guerra
ward *(hospital)* il reparto
warm caldo(a)
it's warm fa caldo
to wash lavare
(to wash oneself) lavarsi
wasp la vespa
watch l'orologio *(m)*
to watch guardare
water l'acqua *(f)*
way in l'entrata *(f)* ; l'ingresso *(m)*
way out l'uscita *(f)*
to wear portare
weather il tempo
weather forecast le previsioni del tempo
website il sito web
wedding il matrimonio
Wednesday mercoledì
week la settimana
last week la settimana scorsa
next week la prossima settimana
per week alla settimana
weekday il giorno feriale
weekend il fine settimana
to weigh pesare
welcome benvenuto
well bene
Welsh gallese
west ovest
wet bagnato(a)
what cosa
what is it? cos'è?
wheel la ruota
wheelchair la sedia a rotelle
when quando
where dove
which qual/quale
white bianco(a)
who chi
whole tutto
why perché
wide largo(a) ; ampio(a)
wife la moglie
to win vincere
wind il vento
window la finestra
(shop) la vetrina
(car) il finestrino
windy: *it's windy* c'è vento
wine il vino
red wine il vino rosso
white wine il vino bianco
winter l'inverno *(m)*
wire il filo
with con
with ice con ghiaccio
with milk con latte
without senza
without ice senza ghiaccio
without milk senza latte
woman la donna
wonderful meraviglioso(a)
wood *(material)* il legno
(forest) il bosco
word la parola
work il lavoro
to work *(person)* lavorare
(machine, car, etc) funzionare
world il mondo
worse peggio
worth *(value)* il valore
it's worth £5 vale cinque sterline
to wrap up *(parcel)* incartare
to write scrivere
wrong sbagliato(a)
what's wrong? cosa c'è?

X

x-ray la radiografia

Y

year l'anno *(m)*
this year quest'anno
next year l'anno prossimo
last year l'anno scorso
yellow giallo(a)
yes sì
yesterday ieri
yet: *not yet* non ancora
young giovane
your il/la suo(a) ; il/la tuo(a) ; il/la vostro(a)

Z

zip la cerniera
zoo lo zoo

Word Zone (Italian-English)

A

a at ; in

abbigliamento *m* clothes

abbonamento *m* subscription ; season ticket

abito *m* dress ; man's suit

abuso *m* misuse

a.C. B.C.

accanto (a) beside ; next (to)

accendere to turn on ; to light

accendino *m* cigarette lighter

acceso(a) on *(light, engine)*

accesso *m* access
divieto di accesso no access

accettazione *f* reception

accomodarsi to make oneself comfortable
si accomodi do take a seat

accordo *m* agreement

aceto *m* vinegar

acqua *f* water
acqua potabile drinking water

addetto(a) person in charge

adesso now

adulto(a) adult

aereo *m* plane ; aircraft

aeroporto *m* airport

affari *mpl* business

affittare to rent ; to let
affittasi for rent

affitto *m* lease ; rent

agenda *f* diary

agenzia *f* agency

aggredire to attack

aglio *m* garlic

ago *m* needle

agosto *m* August

AIDS *m* AIDS

aiutare to help

albergo *m* hotel

albero *m* tree ; mast

alcuni(e) some ; a few

alcuno(a) any ; some

alimentari *mpl* groceries

allacciare to fasten *(seatbelt, etc)*

allergico(a) a allergic to

alloggio *m* accommodation

alpinismo *m* climbing

alt stop

altezza *f* height

alto(a) high ; tall
alta stagione high season

altro(a) other

alzarsi to get up ; to stand up

amare to love *(person)*

amaro(a) bitter *(taste)*

ambasciata *f* embassy

ambiente *m* environment

ambulanza *f* ambulance

ambulatorio *m* surgery ; out-patients

amico(a) *m/f* friend

ammalato(a) ill

ammontare *m* total amount

amore *m* love

analcolico *m* soft drink

analgesico *m* painkiller

anche too ; also ; even

ancora still ; yet ; again

andare to go
andare a piedi to go on foot
andare bene to fit *(clothes)*
andare in macchina to go by car

andata: *andata e ritorno* return *(ticket)*
di (sola) andata single *(ticket)*

andiamo! let's go!

animale *m* animal

anniversario *m* anniversary

anno *m* year
buon anno! happy New Year!

annullare to cancel

annuncio *m* announcement ; advert

anticipo *m* advance *(loan)*
in anticipo in advance ; early

anticoncezionale *m* contraceptive

antifurto *m* burglar alarm

antipasto *m* starter ; hors d'œuvre

antisettico *m* antiseptic

anziano(a) *m/f* senior citizen

aperto(a) open
all'aperto open-air

appartamento *m* flat ; apartment

appuntamento *m* appointment

apribottiglie *m* bottle opener

aprile *m* April

aprire to open ; to turn on *(tap)*

apriscatole *m* tin-opener

arancia *f* orange

arancione orange *(colour)*

area *f* area
area di servizio service area

argento *m* silver

armadio *m* cupboard ; wardrobe

arrabbiato(a) angry

arredato(a) furnished

arrivare to arrive

arrivederci goodbye

arrivo *m* arrival

arrosto *m* roast

arte *f* art ; craft

articolo *m* article

artigiano(a) *m/f* craftsperson

artista *m/f* artist

ascensore *m* lift ; elevator

asciugamano *m* towel

asciugare to dry

ascoltare to listen (to)

aspettare to wait (for) ; to expect

assaggiare to taste

assegno *m* cheque

assicurato(a) insured

assicurazione *f* insurance

assistenza *f* assistance ; aid

assorbenti *mpl* sanitary towels
 assorbenti interni tampons

attendere to wait for

attento(a) careful

attenzione *f* caution
 fare attenzione to be careful

attore *m* actor

attraversare to cross

attraverso through

attrezzatura *f* equipment

attrezzo *m* tool

attrice *f* actress

auguri! best wishes!

aumentare to increase

autista *m/f* driver

auto *f* car

autobus *m* bus

autofficina *f* garage *(for repairs)*

autonoleggio *m* car hire

autore *m* author

autorimessa *f* garage

autostop *m* hitchhiking

autostrada *f* motorway

autunno *m* autumn

avanti in front ; forward(s)
 avanti! come in!

avere to have
 avere bisogno di to need
 avere fame to be hungry
 avere sete to be thirsty

avvisare to inform ; to warn

avviso *m* notice ; advertisement

azienda *f* business ; firm

azzurro(a) light blue

B

babbo *m* daddy
 Babbo Natale Father Christmas

baciare to kiss

bacio *m* kiss

baffi *mpl* moustache

bagaglio *m* luggage

bagnarsi to bathe ; to get wet

bagno *m* bath ; bathroom

ballare to dance

ballo *m* dance

bambino(a) *m/f* child ; baby

bambola *f* doll

banca *f* bank

bancarella *f* stall ; stand

banchina *f* platform ; quay

banco *m* counter ; desk

Bancomat® *m* cash dispenser

banconota *f* banknote

bandiera *f* flag

barattolo *m* tin ; jar

barba *f* beard

barbiere *m* barber

barca *f* boat

basso(a) low ; short

basta that's enough

battello *m* boat

batteria *f* battery *(car)*

baule *m* trunk *(luggage)*

bello(a) beautiful ; fine ; lovely

bene well ; all right ; OK

benvenuto welcome

benzina *f* petrol
 fare benzina to get petrol

bere to drink

bevanda *f* drink

biancheria *f* linen *(for beds, table)*
 biancheria intima underwear

bianco(a) white ; blank

bibita *f* soft drink

bicchiere *m* glass *(for drinking)*

bici *f* bike *(pushbike)*

bicicletta *f* bicycle

bidone *m* bin ; dustbin ; can

biglietteria *f* ticket office

biglietto *m* ticket ; note ; card

binario *m* platform

biologico(a) organic

biondo(a) blond *(person)*

birra *f* beer

biscotto *m* biscuit

bisogno *m* need
 avere bisogno di to need

bistecca *f* steak

bloccare to block

blocco *m* block ; notepad

blu blue

bocca *f* mouth

bolletta *f* bill

bollire to boil

borsa *f* bag ; handbag ; briefcase

borseggiatore *m* pickpocket

borsellino *m* purse ; wallet

bosco *m* wood ; forest

botteghino *m* box office

bottiglia *f* bottle

bottone *m* button

braccialetto *m* bracelet

braccio *m* arm

brindisi *m* toast *(raising glass)*

britannico(a) *f* British

bruciare to burn

brutto(a) bad *(weather, news)* ; ugly

bucato *m* washing ; laundry
 bucato a mano hand washing

buco *m* hole ; leak

buono(a) good
 buon appetito! enjoy your meal!
 a buon mercato cheap

buono *m* voucher ; token

burro *m* butter

bussare to knock *(on door)*

busta *f* envelope

buttare via to throw away

C

cadere to fall

caffè *m* coffee *(espresso)*

calcio *m* football ; kick

caldo(a) hot

calmo(a) calm

calvo(a) bald

calzature *fpl* shoeshop

calze *fpl* stockings

calzini *mpl* socks

calzolaio *m* shoe mender

calzoncini corti *mpl* shorts

cambiare to change

cambio *m* exchange ; gear

camera *f* room *(in house, hotel)*

cameriera *f* chambermaid

cameriere *m* waiter

camicetta *f* blouse

camicia *f* shirt

camion *m* lorry

camminare to walk

campagna *f* countryside ; campaign

campanello *m* bell

campeggio *m* campsite

campione *m* sample ; champion

campo *m* field ; court

camposanto *m* cemetery

canale *m* canal ; channel

cancellare to erase ; to cancel

candela *f* candle ; spark plug

cane *m* dog

canna da pesca *f* fishing rod

cannuccia *f* straw *(for drinking)*

canottiera *f* vest

canotto *m* dinghy *(rubber)*

cantante *m/f* singer

cantare to sing

cantiere *m* building site

cantina *f* cellar ; wine cellar

canzone *f* song

capelli *mpl* hair

capire to understand

capitale *f* capital *(city)*

capo *m* head ; leader ; boss

Capodanno *m* New Year's day

capolavoro *m* masterpiece

capolinea *m* terminus

cappella *f* chapel

cappello *m* hat

cappotto *m* overcoat

carabiniere *m* policeman

caramelle *fpl* sweets

carbone *m* coal ; charcoal

carcere *m* prison

carico *m* load ; shipment ; cargo

carino(a) pretty ; lovely ; nice

carne *f* meat

carnevale *m* carnival

caro(a) dear ; expensive

carrello *m* trolley

carro *m* cart
  carro attrezzi breakdown van

carrozza *f* carriage

carrozzeria *f* bodywork

carta *f* paper ; card ; map
  carta assegni cheque card
  carta di credito credit card
  carta d'identità identity card
  carta igienica toilet paper

carte da gioco *fpl* playing cards

cartello *m* sign ; signpost

cartoleria *f* stationer's

cartolina *f* postcard

casa *f* house ; home
  a casa at home

casco *m* helmet

caso: *in caso di* in case of

cassa *f* till ; cash desk

cassaforte *f* safe *(for valuables)*

castello *m* castle

catena *f* chain

cattedrale *f* cathedral

cattivo(a) bad ; nasty ; naughty

causa *f* cause ; case *(lawsuit)*
  a causa di because of

cavallo *m* horse

cavatappi *m* corkscrew

CD *m* CD

CE *f* EC

celibe *m* single man *(not married)*

cellulare *m* mobile phone

cena *f* dinner *(evening meal)*

cenare to have dinner

cenone *m* New Year's Eve dinner

centesimo *m* cent *(euro)*

centimetro *m* centimetre

centro *m* centre
  centro commerciale shopping centre
  centro storico old town

cercare to look for

cerini *mpl* matches

cerniera *f* zip

cerotto *m* sticking plaster

certificato *m* certificate

cervello *m* brain

che what ; who ; which
  che gusto? what flavour?

chi? who?

chiamare to call

chiamarsi to be called *(name)*

chiave *f* key
  chiave inglese spanner

chiedere to ask ; to ask for

chiesa *f* church

chilo *m* kilo

chilometro *m* kilometre

chiodo *m* nail *(metal)*

chirurgia *f* surgery *(operations)*

chiudere to close ; to turn off
  chiudere a chiave to lock

chiuso(a) closed

ciao! hi! ; bye!

cielo *m* sky

cintura *f* belt
  cintura di sicurezza seatbelt

cioccolato *m* chocolate

circo *m* circus

circolazione *f* traffic

circonvallazione *f* ring road

città *f* city ; town

cittadino(a) citizen

classe *f* class

cliente *m/f* customer

climatizzato(a) air-conditioned

clinica *f* clinic

coda *f* tail ; queue

codice *m* code
  codice postale postcode

cognata *f* sister-in-law

cognato *m* brother-in-law

cognome *m* surname

coincidenza *f* connection *(train)*

colazione *f* breakfast ; lunch

collant *mpl* tights

collega *m/f* colleague

collina *f* hill

collo *m* neck ; package

colomba *f* dove ; Easter cake

colore *m* colour

coltello *m* knife

come like ; as ; how
  come? how? *(in what way)*
  come sta? how are you?
  come va? how's it going?

cominciare to begin

commesso(a) *m/f* assistant ; clerk

commissariato *m* police station

comodo(a) comfortable

compagnia *f* company

compleanno *m* birthday

completo(a) no vacancies ; full

comprare to buy

compreso(a) included

comune *m* town hall ; commune

con with

concerto *m* concert

confermare to confirm

congelatore *m* freezer

congresso *m* conference

conoscere to know

consegna *f* consignment ; delivery

consigliare to advise

consumare to use up

consumazione *f* drink

contanti *mpl* cash

contento(a) happy

continuare to continue

conto *m* account ; bill

contorno *m* vegetable side dish

contratto *m* contract

contro against ; versus

controllare to check

controllo *m* check ; control

convalida *f* date stamp

convalidare to validate *(ticket)*

coperta *f* blanket

coppia *f* couple *(two people)*

corda *f* rope

corpo *m* body

corrente *f* current *(electric, water)*

correre to run

corriere *m* courier

corsa *f* race ; journey

corso *m* course ; avenue

corto(a) short

cos'è? what is it?
  cos'è successo? what happened?

cosa *f* thing
  cosa? what?

così so ; thus *(in this way)*

costare to cost

costoso(a) expensive

costruire to build

costume *m* custom ; costume

cotone *m* cotton
  cotone idrofilo cotton wool

cotto(a) cooked

cravatta *f* tie

credere to believe

credito *m* credit

crema *f* cream ; custard

crescere to grow

croce *f* cross

crociera *f* cruise

cruciverba *m* crossword puzzle

crudo(a) raw

cucchiaino *m* teaspoon

cucchiaio *m* spoon ; tablespoon

cucina *f* cooker ; kitchen ; cooking

cucinare to cook

cucire to sew

cugino(a) *m/f* cousin

cuocere to cook

cuoco *m* chef

cuoio *m* leather

cuore *m* heart

custode *m* caretaker

custodia *f* case ; holder

D

da from ; by ; with ; worth
  da asporto take-away
  dall'Inghilterra from England
  da 100 euro worth 100 euros

danneggiare to spoil ; to damage

dappertutto everywhere

dare to give

data *f* date
  data di nascita date of birth
  data di scadenza sell-by date

dati *mpl* data

davanti a in front of ; opposite

d.C. A.D.

decaffeinato(a) decaffeinated

dente *m* tooth

dentiera *f* dentures

dentifricio *m* toothpaste

dentro in ; indoors ; inside

deposito bagagli *m* left-luggage

descrivere to describe

desiderare to want ; to desire

destra *f* right

detergente *m* cleanser

detersivo *m* detergent

detrazione *f* deduction

dettagli *mpl* details

deviazione *f* detour ; diversion

di of ; some

dialetto *m* dialect

dicembre *m* December

dichiarare to declare

dichiarazione *f* declaration

dieta *f* diet
essere a dieta to be on a diet

dietro behind ; after
dietro di behind

difetto *m* fault

difficile difficult

digerire to digest

dimenticare to forget

Dio *m* God

dipinto(a) painted

dire to say ; to tell

diretto(a) direct

direttore *m* manager ; director

dirigere to manage *(be in charge of)*

diritto(a) straight
sempre diritto straight on

disabile disabled *(person)*

dischetto *m* floppy disk ; diskette

disco *m* disk ; record
disco orario parking disk

disegno *m* drawing

disoccupato(a) unemployed

dispiacere: *mi dispiace* I'm sorry

disponibile available

distaccare to detach ; to unplug

distanza *f* distance

disturbare to disturb

dito *m* finger
dito del piede toe

ditta *f* firm ; company

diurno(a) day(time)

diversi(e) several ; various

diverso(a) different

divertente funny *(amusing)*

divertimento *m* entertainment ; fun

divertirsi to enjoy oneself

divieto forbidden ; not allowed

divisa *f* uniform

divorziato(a) divorced

dizionario *m* dictionary

doccia *f* shower

documenti *mpl* papers *(passport)*

dogana *f* customs

dolce sweet *(not savoury)* ; mild

dolce *m* sweet ; dessert ; cake

dolcificante *m* sweetener

dolore *m* pain ; grief

doloroso(a) painful

domanda *f* question

domandare to ask *(a question)*

domani tomorrow

domenica Sunday

donna *f* woman

dopo after ; afterward(s)

dopodomani the day after tomorrow

doppio(a) double

dormire to sleep

dove? where?

dovere to have to

duomo *m* cathedral

duro(a) hard ; tough ; harsh

E

e and

E east *(abbreviation)*

è is (to be)

ecc. etc.

eccezionale exceptional

ecco here is/are

economico(a) cheap

edicola *f* newsstand ; kiosk

edificio *m* building

effetto *m* effect
effetti personali belongings

egregio(a) dear *(in formal letter)*

elenco *m* list

elettrodomestici *mpl* electrical goods

enoteca *f* wine shop ; wine bar

ente *m* corporation ; body

entrambi(e) both

entrare to come/go in ; to enter

entrata *f* entrance
entrata abbonati season ticket holders' entrance

errore *m* mistake

esame *m* examination

esatto(a) exact ; accurate

esaurito(a) exhausted
tutto esaurito sold out

escluso(a) excluding

esempio example

esercizio *m* exercise ; business

esigenza *f* requirement

esperto(a) expert ; experienced

espresso *m* express train ; coffee

essere to be
essere capace (di) to be able (to)
essere d'accordo to agree
essere nato(a) to be born

est *m* east

estate *f* summer

estero(a) foreign
all'estero abroad

estivo(a) summer

età *f* age

euro euro

euro cent *m* centesimo

Europa *f* Europe

eventuale possible

F

fa ago
un anno fa a year ago

fabbrica *f* factory

fabbricare to manufacture

faccia *f* face

facile easy

fallito(a) bankrupt

fallo *m* foul *(football)*

fame *f* hunger
avere fame to be hungry

famiglia *f* family

fare to do ; to make

farmacia *f* chemist's ; pharmacy

farmaco *m* drug *(medicine)*

faro *m* headlight ; lighthouse

fatto a mano hand-made

fatto di ... made of ...

fattoria *f* farm ; farmhouse

fattura *f* invoice

fazzoletto *m* handkerchief

febbraio February

febbre *f* fever

fede *f* wedding ring

felice happy

femmina *f* female

feriale workday *(Monday-Saturday)*

ferie *fpl* holiday(s)

ferire to injure

ferita *f* wound ; injury ; cut

ferito(a) injured

fermare to stop

fermata *f* stop

fermo(a) still ; off *(machine)*
stare fermo to stay still

ferro da stiro *m* iron *(for clothes)*

ferrovia *f* railway

festa *f* festival ; holiday ; party

festivo(a) sundays/public holiday

fetta *f* slice

fiammifero *m* match

fidanzato(a) engaged *(to marry)*

fiera *f* fair *(trade)*

figlia *f* daughter

figlio *m* son

fila *f* line *(row, queue)*
fare la fila to queue

filiale *f* branch ; subsidiary

filo *m* thread ; wire

finanza *f* finance

fine *f* end
fine stagione end of season

finestra *f* window

finestrino *m* window *(car, train)*

finire to finish

finito(a) finished

fino a until ; as far as

fiori *mpl* flowers

Firenze Florence

firmare to sign

fiume *m* river

foglia *f* leaf *(of tree, etc)*

folla *f* crowd

folle mad
in folle in neutral *(car)*

fonte *f* source

foratura *f* puncture

forbici *fpl* scissors

forchetta *f* fork *(for eating)*

formaggio *m* cheese

fornaio *m* baker

fornello *m* stove ; hotplate

forno *m* oven

forse perhaps

forte strong ; loud ; high *(speed)*

fortunato(a) lucky

forza *f* strength ; force

foto *f* photo

fotocamera digitale *f* digital camera

fototessera *f* passport-type photo

fra between ; among(st)
fra 2 giorni in 2 days

fragile breakable

fragola *f* strawberry

francobollo *m* stamp

fratello *m* brother

frazione *f* village

freccia *f* indicator *(car)* ; arrow

freddo(a) cold

frenare to brake

freno *m* brake

fretta *f* hurry
avere fretta to be in a hurry

frigorifero *m* refrigerator

fritto(a) fried

fronte *f* forehead ; front
di fronte a facing ; opposite

frutta *f* fruit

fruttivendolo *m* greengrocer

fuggire to escape

fulmine *m* lightning

fumare to smoke

fumo *m* smoke

funghi *mpl* mushrooms

funzionare to work *(mechanism)*
non funziona it doesn't work

fuoco *m* fire ; focus
fuochi d'artificio fireworks

fuori outside ; out
fuori servizio out of order

furgone *m* van

furto *m* theft

G

gabinetto *m* lavatory

galleria *f* tunnel ; gallery ; arcade

Galles *m* Wales

gallese Welsh

gamba *f* leg

gara *f* race *(sport)*

gasolio *m* diesel

gassato(a) fizzy

gatto *m* cat
gelato *m* ice cream
geloso(a) jealous
gemelli *mpl* twins ; cufflinks
genere *m* kind *(type)* ; gender
genero *m* son-in-law
genitori *mpl* parents
gentile kind *(person)*
gettare to throw
gettone *m* token
ghiaccio *m* ice
ghiacciolo *m* ice lolly
giacca *f* jacket
giallo *m* thriller *(book or film)*
giallo(a) yellow ; amber *(light)*
giardino *m* garden
ginocchio *m* knee
giocare to play ; to gamble
giocattolo *m* toy
gioco *m* game
gioielli *mpl* jewellery
giornalaio *m* newsagent
giornale *m* newspaper
giornata *f* day
giorno *m* day
giovane young
giovedì *m* Thursday
girare to turn ; to spin
giro *m* tour ; turn
gita *f* trip ; excursion
giù down ; downstairs
giugno *m* June
giusto(a) fair ; right *(correct)*
goccia *f* drop *(of liquid)* ; drip
gola *f* throat ; gorge
gomma *f* rubber ; tyre
gonfio(a) swollen
gonna *f* skirt
gradino *m* step ; stair
Gran Bretagna *f* Great Britain
grande large ; great ; big
grande magazzino *m* department store
grasso(a) fat ; greasy
gratis free of charge
grattugiato(a) grated
gratuito(a) free of charge
grave serious
grazie thank you
gridare to shout
grigio(a) grey
griglia *f* grill
grosso(a) big ; thick
guadagnare to earn
guanto *m* glove
guardare to look (at) ; to watch
guardaroba *m* cloakroom
guardia *f* guard
guasto out of order
guerra *f* war
guida *f* guide
guidare to drive ; to steer
guidatore *m* driver
gustare to taste ; to enjoy
gusto *m* flavour

H

ha...? do you have...?
hotel *m* hotel

I

identificare to identify
idraulico *m* plumber
ieri yesterday
imbarco *m* boarding
imbucare to post *(letter, etc)*
immondizie *fpl* rubbish
imparare to learn
impermeabile *m* raincoat
impiegato(a) *m/f* employee ; white-collar worker
importare to import ; to matter
non importa it doesn't matter
importo *m* (total) amount
in in ; to
in Spagna to Spain
in vacanza on holiday
incaricarsi di to take charge of
incartare to wrap up *(parcel)*
incassare to cash *(a cheque)*
incendio *m* fire
inchiostro *m* ink
incidente *m* accident
incinta pregnant
incluso(a) included ; enclosed
incontrare to meet
incrocio *m* crossroads ; junction
indicazioni *fpl* directions
indice *m* index ; contents
indietro backwards ; behind
indirizzo *m* address
infarto *m* heart attack
infatti in fact ; actually
infermiera *f* nurse
infezione infection
infiammazione *f* inflammation
informazioni *fpl* information
Inghilterra *f* England
inghiottire to swallow
inglese English
ingorgo *m* blockage ; hold-up
ingresso *m* entry/entrance
iniezione *f* injection
inizio *m* start
inoltre besides
inquinato(a) polluted
insalata *f* salad
insegnante *m/f* teacher
insegnare to teach
inserire to insert
insetto *m* insect
insieme together
insieme *m* whole outfit

insolazione *f* sunstroke

interessante interesting

Internet *m* Internet

interno *m* inside

intero(a) whole

interruttore *m* switch

intervento *m* operation

intervista *f* interview

intestato(a) a registered in the name of

intorno around

inutile unnecessary ; useless

invalido(a) disabled ; invalid

invece di instead of

inverno *m* winter

investire to knock down *(car)*

inviare to send

invito *m* invitation

iscritto *m* member
  per iscritto in writing

iscriversi a to join *(club)*

isola *f* island

istruzioni *fpl* instructions

itinerario *m* route

IVA *f* VAT

J

jolly *m* joker *(cards)*

L

là there

labbra *fpl* lips

ladro *m* thief

lago *m* lake

lampadina *f* lightbulb

lana *f* wool

largo(a) wide ; broad

lasciare to leave ; to let *(allow)*

latte *m* milk

lavaggio *m* washing

lavanderia *f* laundry *(place)*

lavandino *m* sink

lavare to wash

lavarsi to wash *(oneself)*

lavasecco *m* dry-cleaner's

lavastoviglie *f* dishwasher

lavatrice *f* washing machine

lavorare to work *(person)*

lavoro *m* job ; occupation ; work

legge *f* law

leggere to read

leggero(a) light *(not heavy)* ; weak

legno *m* wood *(material)*

lentamente slowly

lente *f* lens *(of glasses)*

lenzuolo *m* sheet *(bed)*

lettino *m* cot

letto *m* bed

lettore CD *m* CD player

lì there *(over there)*

libero(a) free/vacant

libreria *f* bookshop

libro *m* book

licenza *f* licence ; permit

limone *m* lemon

lingua *f* language ; tongue

liquori *mpl* spirits *(alcohol)*

liscio(a) straight ; smooth

listino prezzi *m* price list

litro *m* litre

livello *m* level

locale *m* room ; place ; local train

locanda *f* inn

lontano(a) far

lucchetto *m* padlock

luce *f* light

luglio *m* July

luna *f* moon
  luna di miele honeymoon

lunedì *m* Monday

lunghezza *f* length

lungo(a) long

luogo *m* place

lusso *m* luxury

M

ma but

macchia *f* stain ; mark

macchina *f* car ; machine

macellaio *m* butcher's

madre *f* mother

maggio *m* May

maggiore larger ; greater ; older ; largest ; greatest ; oldest

maglietta *f* t-shirt

maglione *m* jumper ; sweater

magro(a) thin *(person)* ; low-fat ; lean *(meat)*

mai never ; ever

maiale *m* pig ; pork

malato(a) ill ; sick

malattia *f* disease

male badly *(not well)*

male *m* pain ; ache

mamma *f* mum(my)

mancia *f* tip *(to waiter, etc)*

mandare to send

mangiare to eat

manica *f* sleeve
  la Manica the English Channel

mano *f* hand

manzo *m* beef

marcia *f* gear *(car)* ; march

marciapiede *m* pavement

mare *m* sea ; seaside

marito *m* husband

marmellata *f* jam

marrone *m* brown ; chestnut

martedì *m* Tuesday
  martedì grasso Shrove Tuesday

marzo *m* March

maschera *f* mask ; fancy dress

maschile masculine ; male

materasso *m* mattress

matrimonio *m* wedding

mattina *f* morning

matto(a) mad

medico *m* doctor

meglio better ; best
meglio di better than

mela *f* apple

meno less ; minus

mensile monthly

menta *f* mint

mentre while ; whereas

menù *m* menu
menù a prezzo fisso set-price menu

meraviglioso(a) wonderful

mercatino dell'usato *m* flea market

mercato *m* market

merci *fpl* freight ; goods

mercoledì *m* Wednesday

merenda *f* snack

meridionale southern

mese *m* month

messa *f* mass *(in church)*

mestruazioni *fpl* period *(menstrual)*

metà *f* half

metro *m* metre

metropolitana *f* underground

mettere to put ; to put on *(clothes)*

mezzanotte *f* midnight

mezzi *mpl* means ; transport

mezzo *m* middle

mezzo(a) half
mezza pensione half board

mezzogiorno *m* midday ; noon
il Mezzogiorno the south of Italy

mezz'ora *f* half an hour

migliore better ; best

miliardo *m* billion

milione *m* million

mille thousand

minorenne underage

minuto *m* minute

misto(a) mixed

mittente *m/f* sender

mobili *mpl* furniture

moderno(a) modern

modo *m* way ; manner

modulo *m* form *(document)*

moglie *f* wife

molti(e) many

molto much ; a lot ; very
molto tempo for a long time
molta gente lots of people

moneta *f* coin ; currency

montagna *f* mountain

morire to die

morsicato(a) bitten

morto(a) dead

mosca *f* fly

moscerino *m* midge ; gnat

mosso(a) rough *(sea)* ; ruffled

mostra *f* exhibition

mostrare to show

moto *f* motorbike

motore *m* engine ; motor

motorino *m* moped

multa *f* fine *(to be paid)*

municipio *m* town hall

muro *m* wall

museo *m* museum

mutande *fpl* underpants

mutandine *fpl* knickers ; panties

N

N north *(abbreviation)*

Napoli Naples

nascita *f* birth

naso *m* nose

nastro *m* tape ; ribbon

nato(a) born

nave *f* ship

né ... né neither ... nor

nebbia *f* fog

negozio *m* shop

nero(a) black

nessuno(a) no ; nobody ; none

neve *f* snow

nevicare to snow

niente nothing

nipote *m/f* nephew/niece

nipotina *f* granddaughter

nipotino *m* grandson

nocivo(a) harmful

nodo *m* knot ; bow

noleggiare to hire

noleggio *m* hire

nome *m* name ; first name

non not
non ancora not yet

nonna *f* grandmother

nonno *m* grandfather

nord *m* north

notare to notice

notizie *fpl* news

notte *f* night

novembre *m* November

nubile single *(woman)*

nulla nothing ; anything

numero *m* number ; size *(of shoe)*

nuora *f* daughter-in-law

nuotare to swim

nuovo(a) new
di nuovo again

nuvoloso(a) cloudy

O

o or

O west *(abbreviation)*

obbligatorio(a) compulsory

occasione *f* opportunity ; bargain

occhiali *mpl* glasses

occhio *m* eye

occupato(a) busy ; engaged

officina *f* workshop ; repair shop

oggi today

ogni each ; every
  ogni giorno every day ; daily
  ogni tanto occasionally
olio *m* oil
olive *fpl* olives
oltre beyond ; besides
ombra *f* shade
ombrello *m* umbrella
ombrellone *m* sun umbrella
onde *fpl* waves
opuscolo *m* brochure
ora now
ora *f* hour
  ora di punta rush hour
orario *m* timetable
  in orario on time
ordinare to order ; to prescribe
ordine *f* order *(in restaurant)*
ordinato(a) tidy
orecchini *mpl* earrings
orecchio *m* ear
oro *m* gold
orologio *m* clock ; watch
ospedale *m* hospital
ospite *m/f* guest ; host/hostess
osso *m* bone
ostello *m* hostel
  ostello della gioventù youth hostel
ottenere to get ; obtain
ottimo(a) excellent
ottobre *m* October
ovest *m* west

P

pacchetto *m* packet
padre *m* father
padrone(a) *m/f* owner
paesaggio *m* scenery ; countryside
paese *m* country *(nation)* ; village
pagare to pay ; to pay for
pagato(a) paid
paio *m* pair
palazzo *m* building ; palace
palla *f* ball
pallina *f* ball *(small)*
pallone *m* football
pane *m* bread ; loaf
panificio *m* bakery
panino *m* bread roll
paninoteca *f* sandwich bar
panna *f* cream
pannolini *mpl* nappies
pantaloni *mpl* trousers
  pantaloni corti shorts
pantofole *fpl* slippers
papa *m* pope
papà *m* daddy
parcheggio *m* car park
parco *m* park
parente *m/f* relation ; relative
parlare to speak ; to talk
parola *f* word
  parola d'ordine password
parolaccia *f* swear word
parrucchiere(a) *m/f* hairdresser
parte *f* share ; part ; side
partire to depart ; to leave
partita *f* match ; game
passaggio *m* passage ; lift *(in car)*
  dare un passaggio to give a lift
passeggiata *f* walk ; stroll
passeggino *m* pushchair
passo *m* pace ; pass *(mountain)*
  fare quattro passi to go for a stroll
pasticcino *m* cake *(small, fancy)*
pastiglia *f* tablet *(pill)*
pasto *m* meal
patata *f* potato
patatine *fpl* crisps
  patatine fritte chips
patente *f* permit ; driving licence
pavimento *m* floor
pedaggio *m* toll *(motorway)*
pedoni *mpl* pedestrians
peggio worse
pelle *f* skin ; hide ; leather
pellicola *f* film *(for camera)*
pelo *m* fur
penna *f* pen
pensare to think
pensione *f* guesthouse
  pensione completa full board
  mezza pensione half board
pepe *m* pepper *(spice)*
per for ; per ; in order to
pera *f* pear
perché why ; because ; so that
percorso *m* walk ; journey ; route
perdere to lose ; to miss *(train, etc)*
perdita *f* leak *(of gas, liquid)*
pericolo *m* danger
pericoloso(a) dangerous
periferia *f* outskirts ; suburbs
permanenza *f* stay ; residency
permesso *m* licence ; permit
  permesso! excuse me! *(to get by)*
perso(a) lost *(object)* ; missed
persona *f* person
pesare to weigh
pesca *f* angling ; fishing ; peach
pescare to fish
pesce *m* fish
pesche *m* peaches
pescivendolo *m* fishmonger's
peso *m* weight
pettine *m* comb
petto *m* chest ; breast
pezzo *m* piece ; bit ; cut *(of meat)*
piacere to please
  piacere! pleased to meet you!
piangere to cry *(weep)*
piano slowly ; quietly
piano *m* floor *(of building)* ; plan
pianta *f* map ; plan ; plant
pianterreno *m* ground floor

piantina *f* street map

piatto *m* dish ; course ; plate

piazza *f* square *(in town)*

piccante spicy ; hot

piccolo(a) little ; small

piede *m* foot
  a piedi on foot

pieno(a) full

pigro(a) lazy

pila *f* battery ; torch

pillola *f* pill

pioggia *f* rain

piombo *m* lead *(metal)*

piovere to rain

piscina *f* swimming pool

pista *f* track ; race track

più more ; most ; plus
  più tardi later

plastica *f* plastic

pneumatico *m* tyre

po' a little *(shortened form of* poco*)*

pochi(e) few

poco(a) little ; not much
  un po' a little

poi then

polizia *f* police

pollo *m* chicken

polmone *m* lung

pomeriggio *m* afternoon

pomodoro *m* tomato

pompa *f* pump

ponte *m* bridge ; deck

pontile *m* jetty ; pier

porta *f* door ; gate ; goal

portabagagli *m* luggage rack

portacenere *m* ashtray

portafoglio *m* wallet

portare to carry/bring ; to wear

portineria *f* caretaker's lodge

porto *m* port ; harbour

posate *fpl* cutlery

posta *f* post office ; mail

posto *m* place ; job ; seat

potabile ok to drink

potere to be able

pranzo *m* lunch

preavviso *m* advance notice

preferito(a) favourite

prefisso *m* prefix ; area code

pregare to pray
  si prega... please...

prego don't mention it!

premere to push ; to press

premio *m* prize

prendere to take ; to catch *(bus)*

prenome *m* first name

prenotare to book ; to reserve

prenotato(a) reserved

prenotazione *f* reservation

preoccupato(a) worried

presa *f* socket *(electric)*

preservativo *m* condom

prestare to lend

presto early ; soon

prete *m* priest

previsione *f* forecast

previsto(a) scheduled ; expected

prezzo *m* price

prima di before

primavera *f* spring *(season)*

primo(a) first ; top ; early
  primo piano first floor
  primo piatto first course

principiante *m/f* beginner

professore *m/f* teacher ; professor

profondo(a) deep

progettare to plan

proibire to ban ; to prohibit

proibito(a) forbidden ; prohibited

promettere to promise

pronto(a) ready
  pronto! hello! *(on telephone)*
  pronto soccorso casualty

proprietario(a) *m/f* owner

proprio(a) own

prosciutto *m* ham

prossimo(a) next

provare to try ; to test *(try out)*

provvisorio(a) temporary

pubblicità *f* advertisement

pulito(a) clean

pullman *m* coach

punteggio *m* score

punto *m* point ; stitch ; full stop

puntura *f* bite ; sting ; injection

puzzo *m* bad smell

Q

qua here

quaderno *m* exercise book

quadro *m* picture ; painting

qual(e) what ; which ; which one

qualche some
  qualche volta sometimes

qualcosa something ; anything

qualcuno someone ; somebody

qualsiasi any

qualunque any

quando? when?

quanto(a)? how much?
  quanti(e)? how many?

quartiere *m* district

quarto *m* quarter

quattro four

quel(la)(lo) that ; that one

questo(a) this ; this one

questura *f* police station

qui here

quindi then ; therefore

quindici giorni fortnight

quotidiano(a) daily

R

rabbia *f* anger ; rabies

racconto *m* story

radio *f* radio

radiografia *f* x-ray

raffreddore *m* cold *(illness)*

ragazza *f* young woman ; girlfriend

ragazzo *m* young man ; boyfriend

rallentare to slow down

rapido(a) high-speed ; quick

rasoio *m* razor

reclamo *m* complaint

regalo *m* present ; gift

reggiseno *m* bra

registrare to record

Regno Unito *m* United Kingdom

regolare regular ; steady

rendersi conto di to realize

reparto *m* department ; ward

restare to stay ; to remain

restituire to return ; to give back

resto *m* remainder ; change

rete *f* net ; goal

retro *m* back

ricambio *m* spare part ; refill

ricaricare to recharge *(battery)*

ricetta *f* prescription ; recipe

ricevuta *f* receipt

richiedere to require

richiesta *f* request

riciclare to recycle

riconoscere to recognize

ricordare to remember

ricordo *m* souvenir ; memory

ridere to laugh

riduttore *m* adaptor

riduzione *f* reduction

riempire to fill

rientro *m* return ; return home

rifiutare to refuse

rifiuti *mpl* rubbish ; waste

rigore *m* penalty *(football)*

riguardo *m* care ; respect
  riguardo a... regarding...

rimandare to postpone

rimanere to stay ; to remain

rimborso *m* refund

rimettersi to recover *(from illness)*

rimorchiare to tow

Rinascimento *m* Renaissance

rinfreschi *mpl* refreshments

ringraziare to thank

rinnovare to renew

rinunciare to give up

riparare to repair

riparato(a) sheltered ; repaired

riparazione *f* repair

ripetere to repeat

riposarsi to rest

riposo *m* rest *(repose)*

riscaldamento *m* heating

riscaldare to heat up *(food)*

riscuotere to collect ; to cash

riservare to reserve

riservato(a) reserved

riso *m* rice ; laugh

risparmiare to save *(money)*

rispondere to answer ; to reply

risposta *f* answer

ristorante *m* restaurant

ritardo *m* delay

ritiro *m* retirement ; withdrawal

ritornare to return *(go back)*

riunione *f* meeting

riuscita *f* result ; outcome

rivista *f* magazine ; revue

roba *f* stuff ; belongings

romanzo *m* novel

rompere to break

rosa pink

rosso(a) red

rotonda *f* roundabout

rotto(a) broken

roulotte *f* caravan

rovesciare to spill ; to knock over

rubare to steal

rubinetto *m* tap

rubrica *f* address book

ruggine *f* rust

rullino *m* roll of film

rumore *m* noise

ruota *f* wheel

S

S south *(abbreviation)*

sabato Saturday

sabbia *f* sand

sacco *m* large bag
  sacco a pelo sleeping bag
  sacco della spazzatura bin bag

sala *f* hall ; auditorium
  sala da pranzo dining room

salario *m* wage

salato(a) salted ; savoury

saldi sale

saldo *m* payment ; balance

sale *m* salt

salire to rise ; to go up

salita *f* climb ; slope

salotto *m* living room ; lounge

salsa *f* sauce

saltato(a) sautéed

salute *f* health
  salute! cheers!

saluto *m* greeting

salvare to rescue ; to save *(life)*

salve! hello!

salvo except ; unless

sangue *m* blood

sapere to know

sapone *m* soap

sapore *m* flavour ; taste

sarto *m* tailor

sbagliato(a) wrong

sbaglio *m* mistake

scadenza *f* expiry

scadere to expire *(ticket, etc)*

scaduto(a) out-of-date ; expired

scala *f* scale ; ladder ; staircase

scaldare to heat up

scale *fpl* stairs

scannerizzare to scan
lo scan scan
lo scanner scanner

scarico(a) flat *(battery)*

scarpa *f* shoe

scarponcini *mpl* walking boots

scatola *f* box ; tin

scegliere to choose

scelta *f* range ; selection ; choice

scendere to go down
scendere da to get off *(bus, etc)*

scheda *f* slip *(of paper)* ; card
scheda telefonica phonecard

schiena *f* back *(of body)*

sciare to ski

sciarpa *f* scarf

sciogliere to melt

sciopero *m* strike

scivolare to slip

scomodo(a) inconvenient ; uncomfortable

scomparire to disappear

sconto *m* discount

scontrino *m* ticket ; receipt ; chit

scorso(a) last

scottatura *f* burn

scrivania *f* desk

scrivere to write ; to spell

scuola *f* school

scuro(a) dark *(colour)*

scusarsi to apologise

scusi? pardon?

se if ; whether

secondo *m* second *(time)* ; main course *(meal)*

secondo(a) second ; according to

sede *f* head office

sedersi to sit down

sedia *f* chair
sedia a rotelle wheelchair

segnare to score *(goal)*

seguente following

seguire to follow ; to continue

selvatico(a) wild

semaforo *m* traffic lights

seminterrato basement

semplice plain ; simple

sempre always ; ever
per sempre for ever

sentiero *m* path ; footpath

sentire to hear

sentirsi to feel

senza without

sera *f* evening

servire to serve

servizio *m* service ; report *(in press)*

servizi *mpl* facilities ; bathroom

seta *f* silk

sete *f* thirst
avere sete to be thirsty

settembre *m* September

settentrionale northern

settimana *f* week

settimanale weekly

sfuso(a) loose ; on tap *(wine)*

sicurezza *f* safety ; security

sicuro(a) sure

Sig. Mr *abbreviation of* Signor

Sig.ra Mrs/Ms *abbreviation of* Signora

sigaretta *f* cigarette

sigaro *m* cigar

Sig.na Miss *abbreviation of* Signorina

Signor: *il Signor Grandi* Mr Grandi

signora *f* lady ; madam ; Mrs ; Ms
signore ladies

signore *m* gentleman ; sir
signori gents

signorina *f* young woman ; Miss

simpatico(a) pleasant ; nice

sindaco *m* mayor

sinistra *f* left

sistemare to arrange

sito *m* site
sito web website

slegato(a) loose *(not fastened)*

smarrito(a) missing *(thing)*

smettere to stop doing something

soccorso *m* assistance ; help

socio *m* associate ; member

soggiorno *m* stay ; sitting room

soldi *mpl* money

sole *m* sun ; sunshine

solito: *di solito* usually

solo(a) alone ; only

sopra on ; above ; over
di sopra upstairs

sopravvivere to survive

sorella *f* sister

sorpassare to overtake *(in car)*

sorriso *m* smile

sospeso(a) suspended ; postponed

sosta *f* stop

sotterraneo(a) underground

sotto underneath ; under ; below

sparire to disappear

spazzatura *f* rubbish

spazzola *f* brush

spedire to send ; to dispatch

spegnere to turn off ; to put out

spento(a) turned off ; out *(light)*

sperare to hope

spese *fpl* shopping ; expenses

spesso often

spettacolo *m* show ; performance

spiaggia *f* beach ; shore

spiegare to explain

spina *f* bone *(of fish)* ; plug *(electric)*

spingere to push

spogliatoio *m* dressing room

sporco(a) dirty

sportello *m* counter ; window

sportivo(a) informal *(clothes)*

sposarsi to get married

spuntino *m* snack

squadra *f* team

stabilimento *m* factory

stagione *f* season

stanco(a) tired

stanza *f* room

stare to be
  stare attento(a) a... beware of..
  stare bene to be well
  stare in piedi to stand

stasera tonight ; this evening

Stati Uniti *mpl* United States

stazione *f* station ; resort

stella *f* star

stesso(a) same

stirare to iron

stivali *mpl* boots

storia *f* history

storico(a) historic(al)
  centro storico old town

strada *f* road ; street

straniero(a) foreign ; foreigner

strano(a) strange

su on ; onto ; over ; about ; up

subito at once ; immediately

succedere to happen

succo *m* juice

sud *m* south

suocera *f* mother-in-law

suocero *m* father-in-law

suonare to ring ; to play

suono *m* sound

superare to exceed ; to overtake

surgelato(a) frozen

sveglia *f* alarm clock/call

svegliare to wake up

svenire to faint

sviluppare to develop *(photos)*

T

tabaccaio *m* tobacconist's

tacco *m* heel

taglia *f* size *(of clothes)*

tagliare to cut

tailleur *m* women's suit

tangenziale *f* by-pass

tanti(e) so many

tanto(a) so much ; so

tappo *m* cork ; plug ; cap

tardi late

targa *f* numberplate *(car)*

tasca *f* pocket

tasso *m* rate

tavola *f* table ; plank ; board

tazza *f* cup

tè *m* tea

tedesco(a) German

telecomando *m* remote control

telefonare to (tele)phone

telefonino *m* mobile phone

telefono *m* telephone

tempesta *f* storm

tempo *m* weather ; time

temporale *m* thunderstorm

tenda *f* curtain ; tent

tenere to keep ; to hold

terra *f* earth ; ground

terremoto *m* earthquake

terzi *mpl* third party

terzo(a) third

tessera *f* pass ; season ticket

tesserino *m* pass *(bus, train)*

testa *f* head

tetto *m* roof

Tevere *m* Tiber

tirare to pull

toccare to touch ; to feel

togliere to remove ; to take away

toilette *f* toilet

topo *m* mouse

Torino *f* Turin

tornare to return ; to come/go back

torneo *m* tournament

toro *m* bull

torre *f* tower

torta *f* cake ; tart ; pie

Toscana *f* Tuscany

tosse *f* cough

tovaglia *f* tablecloth

tra between ; among(st) ; in

tradurre to translate

traduzione *f* translation

traghetto *m* ferry

tramezzino *m* sandwich

trasferire to transfer

trasporto *m* transport

trattoria *f* restaurant

traversata *f* crossing ; flight

treno *m* train

trimestre *m* term *(school)*

triste sad

troppi(e) too many

troppo too much ; too

trovare to find

tubo *m* pipe ; tube

tuffarsi to dive

turno *m* turn ; shift
  di turno on duty

tutti(e) all ; everybody

tutto everything ; all

U

uccello *m* bird

uccidere to kill

UE European Union

ufficio *m* office ; church service

uguale equal ; even

ultimo(a) last

unghia *f* nail *(finger, toe)*

università *f* university

uomo *m* man
  uomini gents

uova *mpl* eggs

uovo *m* egg

usare to use

uscire to go/come out

uscita *f* exit/gate

uso *m* use

utile useful

uva *f* grapes

V

vacanza *f* holiday(s)

vaglia *m* money order

valanga *f* avalanche

valigia *f* suitcase

valore *m* value; worth
  di valore valuable

vasetto *m* jar

vaso *m* vase

vecchio(a) old

vedere to see

vedova *f* widow

vedovo *m* widower

vegetaliano(a) vegan

vegetariano(a) vegetarian

veicolo *m* vehicle

vela *f* sail ; sailing

velenoso(a) poisonous

veloce quick

vendere to sell
  vendesi for sale

vendita *f* sale

venerdì *m* Friday

venerdì santo *m* Good Friday

venire to come

ventaglio *m* fan *(hand-held)*

vento *m* wind

verde green

verdura *f* vegetables

vernice *f* paint

vero(a) true ; real ; genuine

versamento *m* payment ; deposit

vespa *f* wasp

vestirsi to get dressed

vestito *m* dress

vetrina *f* shop window

vetro *m* glass *(substance)*

via *f* street ; by *(via)*

viaggiare to travel

viaggio *m* journey ; trip ; drive

vicino (a) near ; close by

vicolo *m* alley ; lane

videogioco *m* computer game

vietato forbidden
  vietato l'ingresso no entry

vigili del fuoco fire brigade

vigilia *f* eve
  Vigilia di Natale Christmas Eve

vigna *f* vineyard

vincere to win

vino *m* wine

violentare to rape

visita *f* visit

visitare to visit

vista *f* view

visto *m* visa

vita *f* life ; waist

vite *f* vine ; screw

vivere to live

vivo(a) live ; alive

volare to fly

volere to want

volo *m* flight

volta *f* time
  una volta once
  due volte twice

vuoto(a) empty

Z

zanzara *f* mosquito

zia *f* aunt

zio m uncle

zucchero *m* sugar

Reference Zone

This section gives you the nuts and bolts – everything from alphabet and numbers to telling the time, plus the grammar bits including nouns, adverbs, pronouns and verb tables. Each topic has its own track and is illustrated with examples.

Alphabet (a, b, c)

The Italian alphabet contains the same letters as the English alphabet, though some letters are much less common than in English, or are found only in 'borrowed' words of English origin, such as **il software** and **il brandy**. The letters which are rarely used are: j, k, w, x, and y. Vowels can also have accents: **à, è, é, ì, ò, ù**.

a	*a*	n	***en**-nay*
b	*bee*	o	*o*
c	*tchee*	p	*pee*
d	*dee*	q	*koo*
e	*ay*	r	***er**-ray*
f	***ef**-fay*	s	***es**-say*
g	*djee*	t	*tee*
h	***ak**-ka*	u	*oo*
i	*ee*	v	*vee* or *voo*
j	*ee **loon**-ga*	w	*voo **dop**-pya*
k	***kap**-pa*	x	*eeks*
l	***el**-lay*	y	***eep**-see-lon*
m	***em**-may*	z	***dzet**-a*

how do you spell it?	**come si scrive?** ***ko**-may see **skree**-vay?*
it's spelt ...	**si scrive ...** *see **skree**-vay ...*
a as in Ancona, b as in Bari	**a come Ancona, b come Bari** *a **ko**-may an-**ko**-na, bee **ko**-may **ba**-ree*
in capital letters/in small letters	**in maiuscolo/in minuscolo** *een ma-**yoo**-sko-lo/een mee-**noos**-ko-lo*
full-stop/comma	**punto/virgola** ***poont**-o/**veer**-go-la*
all one word	**tutta una parola** ***toot**-ta **oo**-na pa-**ro**-la*

need to know

Italian does not use capital letters for days, months, languages and nationalities.

Numbers (1, 2, 3)

These operate the same way in Italian as in English. Some differences occur in how they are written.

In Italian, decimals are written with a comma instead of our full stop (eg 2,5 for 2.5), and where English uses a comma in numbers like 1,000, Italian uses a full stop:

a 1.6 litre engine **un motore da 1,6 litri**
€10,000.00 **€10.000,00**

When reading phone numbers out loud, we tend to say each number: (o-one-four-one ...) but Italian likes to group them in a variety of ways. A common way is in groups of two digits, so that the local phone number: 291347 would be **ventinove**, **tredici**, **quarantasette**. If you include the area code, the numbers of the code are expressed singly, so that 06 (code) 745082 would be **zero sei**, **settantaquattro**, **cinquanta**, **ottantadue**.

0	**zero** ***dzer***-*o*
1	**uno** ***oo***-*no*
2	**due** ***doo***-*ay*
3	**tre** *tray*
4	**quattro** ***kwat***-*tro*
5	**cinque** ***tcheen***-*kway*
6	**sei** ***say***-*ee*
7	**sette** ***set***-*tay*
8	**otto** ***ot***-*to*
9	**nove** ***nov***-*ay*
10	**dieci** *dee*-***ay***-*tchee*
11	**undici** ***oon***-*dee-tchee*
12	**dodici** ***dod***-*ee-tchee*
13	**tredici** ***tred***-*ee-tchee*
14	**quattordici** *kwat*-***tor***-*dee-tchee*
15	**quindici** ***kween***-*dee-tchee*
16	**sedici** ***sed***-*ee-tchee*
17	**diciassette** *dee-tchas*-***set***-*tay*
18	**diciotto** *dee*-***tchot***-*to*
19	**diciannove** *dee-tchan*-***nov***-*ay*
20	**venti** ***ven***-*tee*
21	**ventuno** *ven*-***too***-*no*
22	**ventidue** *ven-tee*-***doo***-*ay*
30	**trenta** ***tren***-*ta*
40	**quaranta** *kwa*-***ran***-*ta*

50	cinquanta	*tcheen-**kwan**-ta*
60	sessanta	*ses-**san**-ta*
70	settanta	*set-**tan**-ta*
80	ottanta	*ot-**tan**-ta*
90	novanta	*nov-**an**-ta*
100	cento	***tchent**-o*
110	cento dieci	***tchent**-o-dee-**ay**-chee*
250	duecentocincuanta	***doo**-ay-tchent-o-cheen-**kwan**-ta*
500	cinquecento	***tcheen**-kway-**tchent**-o*
1,000	mille	***meel**-lay*
2,000	duemila	*doo-ay-**mee**-la*
1,000,000	un milione	*oon meel-**yo**-nay*

need to know

Watch out for tricky spellings: 'thousand' is mille but 'thousands' are mila; 'million' is milione, but 'millions' are milioni. Remember to write long numbers joined together.

he lives at number 10	abita al numero dieci ***a**-bee-ta al **noo**-**mer**-o dee-**ay**-tchee*
on page 19	a pagina diciannove *a **pa**-djee-na dee-tchan-**nov**-ay*
in chapter 7	nel capitolo sette *nel ka-**pee**-to-lo **set**-tay*
the year 2006	l'anno duemilasei ***lan**-no doo-ay-**mee**-la-say-ee*
I'm 26	ho ventisei anni *o ven-tee-**say**-ee **an**-nee*

need to know

With people's ages, you have to use the word anni – you can't just say ha otto for 'he's eight', you have to say ha otto anni.

Numbers (1st, 2nd, 3rd)

In grammar terms, these are known as 'ordinals' since they give the order that things come in. They are also adjectives, but unlike most adjectives in Italian they come before the noun.

Apart from 1st to 10th, Italian ordinals end in **-esimo**. Remember, that because they are adjectives, they agree with the gender of the noun they go with, eg **la prima strada** 'the first street'.

1st/1°	**primo** ***pree***-*mo*
2nd/2°	**secondo** *sek*-***on***-*do*
3rd/3°	**terzo** ***tert***-*so*
4th/4°	**quarto** ***kwar***-*to*
5th/5°	**quinto** ***kween***-*to*
6th/6°	**sesto** ***ses***-*to*
7th/7°	**settimo** ***set***-*tee-mo*
8th/8°	**ottavo** *ot*-***ta***-*vo*
9th/9°	**nono** ***non***-*o*
10th/10°	**decimo** ***detch***-*ee-mo*
11th/11°	**undicesimo** *oon-dee*-***tchez***-*ee-mo*
12th/12°	**dodicesimo** *dod-ee*-***tchez***-*ee-mo*
13th/13°	**tredicesimo** *tred-ee*-***tchez***-*ee-mo*
14th/14°	**quattordicesimo** *kwat-tor-dee*-***tchez***-*ee-mo*
15th/15°	**quindicesimo** *kween-dee*-***tchez***-*ee-mo*
16th/16°	**sedicesimo** *sed-ee*-***tchez***-*ee-mo*
17th/17°	**diciassettesimo** *dee-tchas-set*-***tez***-*ee-mo*
18th/18°	**diciottesimo** *dee-tchot*-***tez***-*ee-mo*
19th/19°	**diciannovesimo** *dee-tchan-nov*-***ez***-*ee-mo*
20th/20°	**ventesimo** *ven*-***tez***-*ee-mo*
21st/21°	**ventunesimo** *ven-toon*-***ez***-*ee-mo*
22nd/22°	**ventiduesimo** *ven-tee-doo*-***ez***-*ee-mo*
30th/30°	**trentesimo** *tren*-***tez***-*ee-mo*
100th/100°	**centesimo** *tchen*-***tez***-*ee-mo*

on the first of December	**il primo dicembre** *eel* ***pree***-*mo dee*-***tchem***-*bray*
she came in third	**è arrivata terza** *ay ar-ree*-***va***-*ta* ***tert***-*sa*
we live on the fifth floor	**abitiamo al quinto piano** *ab-eet*-***ya***-*mo al* ***kween***-*to* ***pya***-*no*

Time (telling the time)

When talking about clock time, the words used are **ora** (singular) and **ore** (plural).

Italians regard time as a plural matter, once it's past **one** o'clock. This makes perfect sense, if you think about it: '**it's one** o'clock' is OK, because 'one' is singular, but you can't say '**it's two** o'clock' because 'two' is a plural word. So you have to say '**they are two** o'clock'. So this is what happens: it's one o'clock **è l'una** (literally: 'it is the one') but **sono le due** (literally: 'they are the two') for 'it's two o'clock'.

For times 'past' the hour, you use **e** 'and'. For times 'to' the hour, you use **meno** 'less' or 'minus'. **Mezza** is used for 'half' and **un quarto** is used for 'a quarter':

it's ten past one (one and ten) **è l'una e dieci**
it's half past five **sono le cinque e mezza**
it's a quarter to eleven **sono le undici meno un quarto**

If you want to say 'at' a certain time, instead of 'it's', use **alle** (or **all'** with **una**):

at six (o'clock) **alle sei**

The twenty-four hour clock is used on TV and radio and for railway announcements. The word **ore** is often missed out:

at 1400 **alle (ore) quattordici**
at 2300 **alle (ore) ventitre**

excuse me, what time is it?	**scusi, che ore sono?** ***skoo**-zee kay **o**-ray **so**-no?*
excuse me, do you have the right time?	**scusi, ha l'ora esatta?** ***skoo**-zee a **lo**-ra ez-**at**-ta?*
at what time?	**a che ora?** *a kay **o**-ra?*
am, in the morning	**di mattina** *dee mat-**tee**-na*
pm, in the afternoon	**di pomeriggio** *dee po-mer-**eed**-djo*
in the evening	**di sera** *dee **ser**-a*
at midday (noon)	**a mezzogiorno** *a **med**-zo-djor-no*
at midnight	**a mezzanotte** *a **med**-za-not-tay*

Time (in general)

The word 'time' covers a lot of meanings in English: 'time is money', 'three times', 'from time to time'. These are all different senses of the word which have different translations in Italian.

Time in general is **il tempo**, but a time in the sense of an occasion or repetition is **la volta**:

non ho tempo I haven't got time

la prima/la prossima/l'ultima volta the first/the next/the last time

'In' is translated in two ways (using **fra/tra** or **in**) depending on the meaning:

lo farò fra (or **tra**) **tre giorni** I'll do it in three days (as in 'I'll start in three days' time')

l'ho fatto in due giorni I did it in two days

'Ago' is rendered by the word **fa**:

l'ho fatto tre giorni fa I did it three days ago

'For' and 'since' are expressed using **da**:

imparo l'italiano da due mesi I've been learning Italian for two months

imparo l'italiano da ottobre I've been learning Italian since October

need to know

Notice that da means 'for' and 'since' and that English uses a past tense whereas Italian uses the present.

sometimes	**qualche volta** ***kwal**-kay **vol**-ta*
from time to time	**di tanto in tanto** *dee **tan**-to een **tan**-to*
soon	**fra poco** *fra **po**-ko*
until 8 o'clock	**fino alle otto** ***feen**-o **al**-lay **ot**-to*
before 5.30	**prima delle cinque e mezza** ***pree**-ma **del**-lay **tcheen**-kway ay **med**-za*
after 9.15	**dopo le nove e un quarto** ***dop**-o lay **nov**-ay ay oon **kwar**-to*
early	**presto** ***pres**-to*
late (ie getting on)/later	**tardi/più tardi** ***tar**-dee/pyoo **tar**-dee*

Days of the week

Days of the week are all masculine in Italian, except **domenica** (Sunday), and they are not written with a capital letter. The Italian for 'day' is **il giorno**.

Monday	**lunedì** *loo-ned-**ee***	Friday	**venerdì** *ven-er-**dee***
Tuesday	**martedì** *mar-ted-**ee***	Saturday	**sabato** *sa-**bat**-o*
Wednesday	**mercoledì** *mer-ko-led-**ee***	Sunday	**domenica** *dom-**en**-ee-ka*
Thursday	**giovedì** *djo-ved-**ee***		

To say that something happened/will happen on a certain day, you just name the day on its own:

l'ho visto lunedì I saw him on Monday
mercoledì vado a Parigi on Wednesday I'm going to Paris

If you add the definite article, eg **il lunedì**, you mean every Monday, on Mondays:

la vedo il lunedì I see her on Mondays (ie every Monday)
la domenica vado lì I go there on Sundays (ie every Sunday)

every Friday	**ogni venerdì** ***on**-yee ven-er-**dee***
last Tuesday	**martedì scorso** *mar-ted-**ee skor**-so*
next Friday	**venerdì prossimo** *ven-er-**dee pros**-see-mo*
this Thursday	**questo giovedì** ***kwes**-to djo-ved-**ee***
today	**oggi** ***od**-jee*
tomorrow	**domani** *dom-**a**-nee*
yesterday	**ieri** ***yer**-ee*
which day?	**quale giorno?** *kwa-lay **djor**-no*

Months and seasons

Months are masculine in Italian. Neither months nor seasons are written with a capital letter. 'Month' is **il mese** and 'season' is **la stagione**.

January	**gennaio** *djen-**na**-yo*	July	**luglio** ***lool**-yo*
February	**febbraio** *feb-**bra**-yo*	August	**agosto** *ag-**os**-to*
March	**marzo** ***mar**-tso*	September	**settembre** *set-**tem**-bray*
April	**aprile** *ap-**ree**-lay*	October	**ottobre** *ot-**tob**-ray*
May	**maggio** ***mad**-djo*	November	**novembre** *nov-**em**-bray*
June	**giugno** ***djoon**-yo*	December	**dicembre** *deech-**em**-bray*
spring	**la primavera** *la pree-ma-**ver**-a*	autumn	**l'autunno** *la-oo-**toon**-no*
summer	**l'estate** *les-ta-**tay***	winter	**l'inverno** *leen-**ver**-no*

need to know

For 'first' primo is used. After that due, tre, etc are used. Therefore il cinque marzo can be, in English, 'the 5th of March' or '5 March' or 'March 5/5th'.

Years are expressed as follows (the numbers are not separated in writing):

in 1953 **nel millenovecentocinquantatre**
in 2006 **nel duemilasei**

on the first of July	**il primo luglio** *eel **pree**-mo **lool**-yo*
on the fifth of March	**il cinque marzo** *eel **tcheen**-kway **mart**-so*
in November	**a novembre** *a nov-**em**-bray*
next September	**il prossimo settembre** *eel **pros**-see-mo set-**tem**-bray*

Colours (red, blue, grey)

Colours agree with the noun they describe. Unlike in English, Italian colours follow the noun. So 'green ties' are **cravatte verdi**, not **verdi cravatte**.

black	**nero(a)** ***ner**-o(a)*	pink	**rosa** ***ro**-za*
blue	**blu** or **azzurro(a)** *bloo* or *ad-**zoor**-ro(a)*	purple	**viola** *vee-**o**-la*
brown	**marrone** *mar-**ro**-nay*	red	**rosso(a)** ***ros**-so(a)*
green	**verde** ***ver**-day*	white	**bianco(a)** ***byan**-ko(a)*
grey	**grigio(a)** ***gree**-djo(a)*	yellow	**giallo(a)** ***djal**-lo(a)*
orange	**arancione** *a-ran-**tcho**-nay*		

Rosa, **viola** and **blu** are 'invariable', which means they never change their endings, even in the plural. Generally speaking, **blu** is a darker blue and **azzurro** a lighter blue, but there is a generous overlap. 'Light' is **chiaro** and 'dark' is **scuro**. When these adjectives combine with a colour, to form a phrase such as 'light grey' or 'dark grey', then there is no agreement, so 'lots of dark grey cars' is **molte macchine grigio scuro**.

need to know

If someone has brown hair, the word castano(a), meaning 'chestnut' is used – dei capelli castani.

what colour is it?	**di che colore è?** *dee kay ko-**lor**-ay ay?*
a blue door	**una porta blu** ***oo**-na **por**-ta blu*
the white sheet	**il lenzuolo bianco** *eel len-**swolo** **byan**-ko*
the yellow cups	**le tazze gialle** *lay tats-**say** **djal**-lay*
a light green shirt	**una camicia verde chiaro** ***oo**-na ka-**mee**-tcha **ver**-day **kyar**-o*

Quantities (a kilo, a tin)

Quantities in Italian are followed by **di** 'of'.

a litre of wine	**un litro di vino** *oon **leet**-ro dee **vee**-no*
half a litre of milk	**mezzo litro di latte** *__med__-dzo **leet**-ro dee **lat**-tay*
200 grams of salame	**due cento grammi di salame** *doo-ay **tchen**-to **gram**-mee dee sa-la-may*
half a kilo of cherries	**mezzo chilo di ciliege** *__med__-dzo **kee**-lo dee **tcheel**-yedj-ay*
a kilo of oranges	**un chilo di arance** *oon **kee**-lo dee a-**ran**-tchay*
a bottle of water	**una bottiglia di acqua** *__oo__-na bot-**teel**-ya dee **ak**-wa*
a glass of cognac	**un bicchiere di brandy** *oon beek-**yer**-ay dee **bran**-dee*
a tin of tomatoes	**una scatola di pomodori** *__oo__-na **skat**-o-la dee po-mo-**dor**-ee*
a packet of cigarettes	**un pacchetto di sigarette** *oon pak-**ket**-to dee see-ga-**ret**-tay*
a carton of fruit juice	**un cartone di succo di frutta** *oon kar-**ton**-ay dee **sook**-ko dee **froot**-ta*
a jar of honey	**un vasetto di miele** *oon va-**zet**-to dee **myel**-ay*
a slice of cake	**una fetta di torta** *__oo__-na **fet**-ta dee **tor**-ta*
more ...	**più di ...** *pyoo dee ...*
less ...	**meno di ...** *__men__-o dee ...*
that's enough	**basta così** *__bas__-ta ko-**zee***

need to know

Remember it's always un/uno/una/un'... di

Nouns (cat, dog, Mary)

Nouns are labels for things: 'market', 'cheese', 'morning', 'Mary' and 'London'. Nouns have no gender in English, but in Italian they are either masculine or feminine.

The fact that Italian nouns are either masculine or feminine doesn't mean that the thing itself necessarily has male or female characteristics. The general rule is that nouns ending in **-o** are masculine, nouns ending in **-a** are feminine and those ending in **-e** can be either gender and simply have to be learned. Examples of noun endings include:

libro 'book' is masculine	**giornale** 'newspaper' is masculine
casa 'house' is feminine	**neve** 'snow' is feminine

When there is more than one of something, the plural form is used; in English, this most often means adding an '-s' (markets, mornings, cheeses) though some words have irregular plurals (man/men; sheep/sheep).

In Italian, no **-s** is added but the ending of the noun changes in this way:

Singular	Plural		
-o	**-i**	**gatto/gatti**	cat/cats
-a	**-e**	**tazza/tazze**	cup/cups
-e	**-i**	**nome/nomi**	name/names

There are (naturally) a small number of exceptions to this rule, eg nouns ending in accented **-à** or **è** do not change in the plural (**città** 'city'; **città** 'cities', **un caffè** 'one coffee', **due caffè** 'two coffees') as do 'non-Italian' words, such as **computer** and **sport** which stay the same in the plural. Nor do one syllable words change: **un tè** 'one tea', **due tè** 'two teas', or abbreviated words such as **la foto** for 'photograph', **tre foto** 'three photos'.

Because of the rules for hard and soft versions of Italian **c**, **g** and **sc** (see Pronunciation, pp 10-11) nouns ending in **-ca**, **-co**, **-go**, **-sco**, **-ga** and **-sca** have plural endings written with an added **h**: **-chi**, **-ghi**, **-schi**, **-che**, **-ghe** and **-sche**. Examples include:

banca bank	**banche** banks
lago lake	**laghi** lakes
tasca pocket	**tasche** pockets

If these plurals were not written with the added **h**, then they would be pronounced ***ban**-tchee, **la**-djee and **ta**-shay.*

need to know

Watch out for nouns ending in: -co, -go, -sco, -ca, -ga and -sca which take an h in the plural. There are a very few exceptions, but one is amico 'friend' which becomes amici in the plural.

Articles (the, a)

Articles are the little words that introduce a noun, 'the' (definite article), 'a', 'some' (indefinite articles). These are quite straightforward in English but are rather more complicated in Italian where the article changes according to whether the noun is singular or plural, masculine or feminine. What letter the noun starts with can also make a difference!

The rules about articles in Italian may seem very complicated, but don't be put off. Once you have mastered these very important words, nothing else in Italian grammar will seem so difficult.

The masculine definite article 'the' is **il** (plural **i**) or, before a noun beginning with a vowel or **h**, **l'** (plural **gli**):

> **il treno/i treni** the train/the trains, **il libro/i libri** the book/the books
> **l'articolo/gli articoli** the article/the articles, **l'hotel/gli hotel** the hotel/the hotels

When a masculine noun begins with **z**, **gn** or **s**+consonant, eg **sc-** (**sconto**), **st-** (**studente**), **sp-** (**sport**) then the article is **lo** (plural **gli**):

> **lo zaino/gli zaini** the rucksack/the rucksacks,
> **lo spuntino/gli spuntini** the snack/the snacks

The feminine definite article is more straightforward. It is **la** (plural **le**) or **l'** (plural **le**) before nouns beginning with a vowel:

> **la casa/le case** the house/the houses, **la pizza/le pizze**, **l'opera/le opere**,
> **l'acqua/le acque** the water/the waters

The masculine indefinite singular article 'a' is **un** except for nouns starting with **z**, **gn** or **s** + consonant when it is **uno**.

> **un treno** a train, **un libro** a book, **un articolo** an article, **un hotel** a hotel
> **uno zaino** a rucksack, **uno spuntino** a snack

The plural equivalent of **un** is **dei**. It becomes **degli** for nouns beginning with vowels, **z**, **gn** or **s** + consonant:

> **dei treni** some trains
> **degli zaini** some rucksacks
> **degli articoli** articles

The feminine singular indefinite article is **una**. Before feminine nouns beginning with vowels, it becomes **un'**:

> **una casa** a house
> **un'ape** a bee

Una and **un'** become **delle** before all plural feminine nouns:

> **delle case** some houses
> **delle api** some bees

Adjectives (pretty, tall ...)

Adjectives are 'describing' words that tell you more about a person or thing, such as colour or size.

Italian adjectives have to agree with the gender of the noun they describe. To make an **-o** adjective feminine, change the **-o** to **-a** (eg **rosso - rossa**). Adjectives ending in **-e** (eg **giovane**) can be either masculine or feminine; the ending changes to **-i** in the plural regardless of whether they are masculine or feminine.

masc. sing.	fem. sing.	masc. plur.	fem. plur.	meaning
piccolo	**piccola**	**piccoli**	**piccole**	small
difficile	**difficile**	**difficili**	**difficili**	difficult

Because adjectives and nouns agree with each other in this way, they often have the same endings:

casa rossa red house (both words are feminine singular)
case rosse red houses (both feminine plural)
muro rosso red wall (both masculine singular)
muri rossi red walls (both masculine plural)
cane felice happy dog (both masculine singular)
cani felici happy dogs (both masculine plural)

Watch out, though, adjective and noun don't always 'rhyme' in this way. If you have a noun with **-o/-a** endings together with an adjective with **-e** endings (or vice versa), this is what happens:

muro verde green wall (both words are masculine singular)
muri verdi green walls (both masculine plural)
classe piccola small class (both feminine singular)
classi piccole small classes (both feminine plural)

The endings will also agree in such sentences as:

la casa è rossa the house is red
le stazioni sono nuove the stations are new

Most Italian adjectives go after the noun they describe, eg 'the red apple' **la mela rossa**. But some very common adjectives usually come before the noun. These are: **bello** 'beautiful', **breve** 'short', **brutto** 'ugly', **buono** 'good', **cattivo** 'bad', **giovane** 'young', **grande** 'big', **lungo** 'long', **nuovo** 'new', **piccolo** 'small', **vecchio** 'old':

a beautiful day **una bella giornata**
a bad man **un cattivo uomo**

Bello and **buono** have slightly different endings from other adjectives before masculine nouns. **Bello** shortens to **bel**, and **buono** to **buon** before masculine singular nouns starting with a consonant: **bel libro**, **bel canto**, **buon vino**, **buon compleanno**; to **bell'** or **buon'** before masculine singular nouns starting with a vowel: **bell'uomo**, **buon'anno**; and to **bello** or **buono** before masculine singular nouns starting with **z**, **gn**, or **s** + consonant: **bello zaino**, **buono stato**. In the plural **bel** becomes **bei**; **bello** and **bell'** become **begli**. **Buono** is regular in the plural.

Possessives (my, mine, yours ...)

These words tell you who is connected with or owns the thing referred to. 'My', 'your', etc are possessive adjectives. 'Mine' and 'yours', etc are possessive pronouns. In Italian the same words are used for both.

Possessives depend on the gender (masculine or feminine) and number (singular or plural) of the noun they accompany, not on the sex of the 'owner', so watch out for **il suo** meaning either 'his' or 'her(s)'.

	with masc. sing. noun	with fem. sing. noun	with masc. plur. noun	with fem. plur. noun
my	**il mio**	**la mia**	**i miei**	**le mie**
your (familiar)	**il tuo**	**la tua**	**i tuoi**	**le tue**
his/her/your formal	**il suo**	**la sua**	**i suoi**	**le sue**
your (plural)	**il vostro**	**la vostra**	**i vostri**	**le vostre**
our	**il nostro**	**la nostra**	**i nostri**	**le nostre**
their	**il loro**	**la loro**	**i loro**	**le loro**

The word for 'the' **il, la, i, le** has to be included:

my book **il mio libro**
their house **la loro casa**
our keys **le nostre chiavi**
his/her pen **la sua penna**

With close family (but singular only) the word for 'the' is omitted in Italian possessives:

my mother **mia madre** (not **la mia madre**)
his sister **sua sorella**

These words are also used as possessive pronouns eg 'mine', 'his', 'theirs' which stand alone, without a noun:

è la mia it's mine (referring to something feminine singular)
dove sono i vostri? where are yours? (referring to something masculine plural)

these keys are mine — **queste chiavi sono le mie**
__kwes__-tay __kya__-vee __so__-no lay __mee__-ay

that's our hotel — **quello è il nostro albergo**
__kwel__-lo ay eel __nos__-tro al-__ber__-go

she's lost her passport — **ha perso il suo passaporto**
a __per__-so eel __soo__-o pas-sa-__por__-to

they can't find their room — **non possono trovare la loro camera**
non __pos__-son-o tro-__va__-ray la __lo__-ro __ka__-mer-a

Demonstratives (this, that ...)

If 'this', 'that' etc are with a noun, they are demonstrative adjectives, eg 'these books are heavy!' or 'I can hear that noise again.'

The adjective 'this' is **questo** (masculine) or **questa** (feminine) and **questi** or **queste** in the plural.

'That' is **quel** (masculine) or **quella** (feminine). The only tricky thing is that **quel** behaves a little like the article **il**, becoming **quello** for nouns beginning with **z**, **gn** or **s** + consonant. And in the plural it drops the **-l** to become **quei** for all masculine plurals except those beginning with vowels or **z**, **gn** and **s** + consonant, when it becomes **quegli**. Feminine **quella** is **quelle** in the plural.

If 'this', 'that', 'these' and 'those' are used on their own, without a noun, they are demonstrative pronouns, eg 'give me *this*' or 'where are *those*?:

	this/that	these/those
masculine	**questo/quello**	**questi/quelli**
feminine	**questa/quella**	**queste/quelle**

Remember to make the pronoun agree with what it is replacing:

gli ho dato questo	I gave him this	(where 'this' refers to something masculine, perhaps a book – **il libro**)
quelle sono le mie	those are mine	(where 'those' refers to something feminine, perhaps keys – **le chiave**)
ha trovato questi!	he found these!	(where 'these' refers to something masculine, perhaps gloves – **i guanti**)

this tree is very big	**quest'albero è molto grande** *kwest-**al**-ber-o ay **mol**-to **gran**-day*
I've got this key	**ho questa chiave** *o **kwes**-ta **kya**-vay*
look at those little houses	**guarda quelle piccole case** ***gwar**-da **kwel**-lay **peek**-ko-lay **ka**-zay*
those dogs are eating	**quei cani mangiano** ***kway**-ee **ka**-nee **man**-dja-no*
that month I was so happy	**quel mese ero così felice** *kwel **mez**-ay **ay**-ro ko-**zee** fel-**ee**-tchay*

Prepositions (in, on, at)

Prepositions in English usually indicate a relationship such as position or time: *in* a small market, *near* the centre *of* Manchester, *at* 8 o'clock.

The only slight difficulty is that the choice of preposition is not always predictable. For example, in English we say 'I'm *on* the train' but in Italian you are 'in' the train: **nel treno** not **sul treno,** which could mean on top of it! Sometimes a preposition is needed in one language but not the other: 'look *at* my car' is just **guarda la mia macchina** but conversely 'I'm phoning your mother' is **telefono *a* tua madre**.

In Italian, some prepositions join up with the definite article which follows them, to form one word: 'to the park' = **a** + **il parco** = **al parco** and 'in the boxes' = **in** + **le scatole** = **nelle scatole**. The prepositions which behave like this are: **a** 'to, at'; **da** 'by, from'; **in** 'in, into'; **su** 'on'; **di** 'of'.

a (to, at)		da (by, from)	
a + il	**= al**	**da + il**	**= dal**
a + lo	**= allo**	**da + lo**	**= dallo**
a + l'	**= all'**	**da + l'**	**= dall'**
a + la	**= alla**	**da + la**	**= dalla**
a + i	**= ai**	**da + i**	**= dai**
a + gli	**= agli**	**da + gli**	**= dagli**
a + le	**= alle**	**da + le**	**= dalle**

su (on)		in (in, into)	
su + il	**= sul**	**in + il**	**= nel**
su + lo	**= sullo**	**in + lo**	**= nello**
su + l'	**= sull'**	**in + l'**	**= nell'**
su + la	**= sulla**	**in + la**	**= nella**
su + i	**= sui**	**in + i**	**= nei**
su + gli	**= sugli**	**in + gli**	**= negli**
su + le	**= sulle**	**in + le**	**= nelle**

in (in, into)		di (of, some)	
in + il	**= nel**	**di + il**	**= del**
in + lo	**= nello**	**di + lo**	**= dello**
in + l'	**= nell'**	**di + l'**	**= dell'**
in + la	**= nella**	**di + la**	**= della**
in + i	**= nei**	**di + i**	**= dei**
in + gli	**= negli**	**di + gli**	**= degli**
in + le	**= nelle**	**di + le**	**= delle**

Di plus the plural article **(dei, delle, degli)** also means 'some':
delle mele 'of the apples' or 'some apples'
degli alberghi 'of the hotels' or 'some hotels'
dei bicchieri 'of the glasses' or 'some glasses'

need to know

Watch out in negative sentences: ho delle mele I've got some apples but non ho mele I haven't got any apples. So, 'some' is di + definite article but 'any' is left untranslated in Italian (I haven't any apples = I haven't apples).

to the hotel	**all' albergo** *al-lal-**ber**-go*
on the cooker	**sulla cucina** ***sool**-la koo-**tchee**-na*
Mary's pen (the pen of Mary)	**la penna di Maria** *la **pen**-na dee ma-**ree**-a*
from my friend	**dal mio amico** *dal **mee**-o a-**mee**-ko*
to the shops	**ai negozi** ***a**-ee neg-**ots**-ee*
in the shade	**all'ombra** *al-**lom**-bra*
Uncle Guido's house	**la casa dello zio Guido** *la **ka**-za **del**-lo **dzee**-o **gweed**-o*
at home	**in casa** *een **ka**-za*

need to know

The preposition con 'with' can also combine with articles: col, cogli, coi, etc. It is becoming increasingly used.

Questions (how? when?)

Italian people ask questions simply by raising the pitch of their voice at the end of the sentence, so that: **ti piace questo** means 'you like this' (a statement) and **ti piace questo?** means 'do you like this?' (a question).

Just as in English, in Italian there are various question words. In English these words often begin with 'wh-', eg 'which' 'why' 'who' etc.

quando?	when?	**che cosa?**	what?
dove?	where?	**quanto(a)?**	how much?
perché?	why?	**quanti(e)?**	how many?
come?	how?	**quale** (plural **quali**)?	which? *or* what?

how many apples?	**quante mele?** ***kwan**-tay **mel**-ay?*
how is he?	**come sta?** ***kom**-ay sta?*
where are you going?	**dove vai?** ***dov**-ay **va**-ee?*
why isn't she coming?	**perché non viene?** *per-**kay** non **vyen**-ay?*
when are we leaving?	**quando partiamo?** ***kwand**-o part-**ya**-mo?*
what are you eating?	**che cosa mangiate?** *kay **ko**-za man-**dja**-tay?*
how much does this computer cost?	**quanto costa questo computer?** *kwan-to kos-ta kwes-to com-**pyoo**-ter?*
who did you see?	**chi hai visto?** *kee **a**-ee **vees**-to?*
which shoes do you prefer?	**quali scarpe preferisci?** ***kwa**-lee **skar**-pay pref-er-**ee**-shee?*

need to know

Che cosa **is often shortened to just** che **or** cosa **in everyday speech:** che c'è? **'what is there?'**; cosa fai? **'what are you doing?'**.

Negatives (no, not, never)

A negative statement or question is one where something is *not* happening, is *not* true, is *not* present.

In Italian, to make something negative, you put 'non' before the verb:

non parlo I don't speak
Paolo non è arrivato Paul hasn't arrived

Statements/questions containing 'never', 'nobody', 'nothing' etc are also negative sentences. Italian uses two negative words for these and the verb goes in the middle:

nothing, not ... anything	**non ... niente**
no-one, nobody, not ... anyone	**non ... nessuno**
never, not ... ever	**non ... mai**
no more, no longer	**non ... più**
not even	**non ... neanche**
neither ... nor	**non ... né ... né**

I never smoke	**non fumo mai** *non **foo**-mo **ma**-ee*
there's nothing here	**non c'è niente qui** *non tchay **nyen**-tay kwee*
I can't see anybody	**non vedo nessuno** *non **ved**-o nes-**soo**-no*
she never arrives on time	**non arriva mai in tempo** *non ar-**ree**-va **ma**-ee een **tem**-po*
he's no longer working here	**non lavora più qui** *non la-**vor**-a pyoo kwee*
we have brought neither pens nor pencils	**non abbiamo portato né penne né matite** *non ab-**ya**-mo por-**tat**-o nay **pen**-nay nay ma-**teet**-ay*
she didn't even pay me	**non mi ha neanche pagato** *non mee a **nyan**-kay pa-**gat**-o*

need to know

Some of these negative words can also be used on their own, in expressions like: chi è venuto? nessuno! 'who came? no one!'; che cosa fai oggi? niente di speciale 'what are you doing today? nothing special'.

Adverbs (slowly, fast)

Adverbs generally describe how something is done. Many adverbs end in -ly in English, eg: she walked *slowly*, we were laughing *happily, unfortunately*, you won't be there.

In Italian, many adverbs end in **-mente**: **lentamente** 'slowly', **sfortunatamente** 'unfortunately'. To form an adverb, the general rule is that you add **-mente** to the feminine form of the adjective:

veloce (masculine and feminine) 'quick', so **velocemente** 'quickly'
attivo (masculine) **attiva** (feminine) 'active', so **attivamente** 'actively'

Watch out for some exceptions: adjectives ending in **-le** lose the **-e** before **-mente**

attuale 'actual', but **attualmente** 'actually'
finale 'final', but **finalmente** 'finally'

A few adjectives just refuse to obey the rule at all, as happens in English too:

buono(a) 'good', but **bene** (not **buonamente**) is 'well' (not 'goodly')
cattivo(a) 'bad', but **male** 'badly'

Important adverbs not ending in **-mente**:

often	**spesso** ***spes***-*so*
ever, never	**mai** ***ma***-*ee*
soon	**fra poco** *fra* ***po***-*ko*
still, yet	**ancora** *an*-***ko***-*ra*
already	**già** *dja*
now	**adesso** *a*-***des***-*so*
maybe	**forse** ***for***-*say*
always	**sempre** ***sem***-*pray*
sometimes	**qualche volta** ***kwal***-*kay* ***vol***-*ta*

need to know

To form an adverb from an adjective in Italian, use the feminine form.

Pronouns (I, me, he)

Pronouns include such words as: I, you, she, they, me, him, them, this, that. A pronoun replaces a noun, to avoid repetition.

	Subject pronouns	Object pronouns	Indirect Object pronouns
I	**io**	me **mi**	to me **mi**
you singular	**tu**	you **ti**	to you **ti**
he/it	**lui**	him/it **lo**	to him **gli**
she/it	**lei**	her/it **la**	to her **le**
you formal	**Lei**	you **La**	to you **Le**
we	**noi**	us **ci**	to us **ci**
you plural	**voi**	you **vi**	to you **vi**
they masculine	**loro**	them **li**	to them **gli/loro**
they feminine	**loro**	them **le**	to them **gli/loro**

Tu is the familiar form for 'you' used when talking to a person you know well or a child; **Lei** is the polite or formal form and is often written with a capital letter.

Italian often omits subject pronouns entirely. This is because the ending of the verb changes from person to person, making it absolutely clear who the subject is, ie who is doing the action. This would never work in English, which is why we find it so mystifying: 'I arrive' is **io arrivo** or just **arrivo** as the **-o** ending tells you it's 'I' who is arriving. And 'we arrive' is **noi arriviamo** or more simply **arriviamo** as the **-iamo** ending tells you it's 'we' who are arriving. The subject pronouns are only used for emphasis or to avoid ambiguity.

Direct object pronouns replace the direct object. They come before the verb in Italian:

we see them **li vediamo**
the dog has followed me **il cane mi ha seguito**

Indirect object pronouns replace expressions using **a** 'to', eg, **a lui** 'to him', **a me** 'to me'. They go before the verb, except for **loro** which follows it:

I'm giving these to you (familiar) **ti do questi**
I write to him **gli scrivo**
I write to them **scrivo loro**

they have given us a present **ci hanno dato un regalo**
*tchee **an**-no **dat**-o oon reg-**a**-lo*

need to know

Object pronouns precede the verb (except loro), unless it's an infinitive, then the pronoun hooks onto the end, eg 'I want to see them' voglio vederli.

Verbs (to be, to see, to do)

Verbs are the words that correspond to the action of a sentence.

The form in which you would look up a verb in the dictionary is known as the infinitive. This is the 'to' part, eg 'to go', 'to finish'. In Italian the infinitive is a single word: **andare** 'to go', **finire** 'to finish'.

Italian verbs are grouped into three main categories according to the ending of that infinitive form, which in the vast majority of cases is either **-are**, **-ere** or **-ire** (these are known as regular verbs). Of course, there are various 'irregular verbs' as well.

The different forms of the verb reflecting time are called tenses: present, future, etc. There are different kinds of past tense: one called the perfect tense tells you about a single complete action that is finished and done with, while the imperfect tense denotes an action that continues over a period of time or was still ongoing when something else happened. We have something similar in English with 'I had a shower and went out' as opposed to 'I was having a shower when the phone rang'. The perfect can also be translated using 'have': 'I have had a shower', 'I have never been to Italy'.

The Italian past tense, for example, 'I have spoken' **ho parlato** or 'I have left' **sono partito**, is formed using the present of **avere** or **essere** and the past participle **parlato**, so **ho parlato**. Verbs that take **essere** are often verbs involving motion such as **andare** 'to go', **venire** 'to come', **arrivare** 'to arrive' and **partire** 'to leave'. When **essere** is used, the past participle must agree with the subject. So 'Maria has left' is **Maria è partita**. And 'we have left' or 'we left' is **siamo partiti**. When there is a mixed goup of people, then the masculine ending is used.

The imperative (command) form is the one you use to give orders ('do this! don't do that!') or make suggestions to a group that includes yourself ('let's do this! let's not do that!'). Here are the forms for the different types of verb, **-are**, **-ere** and **-ire**:

tu (you, familiar singular)	**parla!**	**credi!**	**dormi!**
lei (you, polite singular)	**parli!**	**creda!**	**dorma!**
noi (we)	**parliamo!**	**crediamo!**	**dormiamo!**
voi (you, familiar plural)	**parlate!**	**credete!**	**dormite!**
loro (you, polite plural)	**parlino!**	**credano!**	**dormano!**

For negative commands **non** goes before the imperative form except for **tu** when the infinitive is used: **non andare!** 'don't go!'. For commands involving reflexive verbs, the pronouns get tacked onto the verb: **servitevi** 'help yourselves!', **curati** 'take care of yourself'. For the **tu** negative form, the final **-e** is dropped from the infinitive: **non preoccuparti** 'don't worry'. When the **lei** form is used, the pronoun **si** goes before the verb: **si accomodi** 'sit down', **non si preoccupi** 'don't worry'.

The subjunctive is used in constructions involving an unreal or hypothetical case. It is used after certain expressions which just have to be learnt. Usually there will be a **che** 'that' between the expression and the subjunctive: **voglio che tu sia qui** 'I want you to be here' (literally: 'I want that you should be here').

parlare (-are verb, to speak)

Present	io	**parlo** *__par__-lo*	I don't speak French
	tu	**parli** *__par__-lee*	non **parlo** francese
	lui/lei	**parla** *__par__-la*	*non __par__-lo fran-__tchez__-ay*
	noi	**parliamo** *parl-__ya__-mo*	
	voi	**parlate** *par-__la__-tay*	
	loro	**parlano** *__par__-lan-o*	
Past: perfect		**ho parlato** *o par-__lat__-o*	I spoke to your brother yesterday
		hai parlato *__a__-ee par-__lat__-o*	ho **parlato** con tuo fratello ieri
		ha parlato *a par-__lat__-o*	*o par-__lat__-o kon __too__-o frat-__tel__-lo __yer__-ee*
		abbiamo parlato *ab-__ya__-mo par-__lat__-o*	
		avete parlato *a-__vet__-ay par-__lat__-o*	
		hanno parlato *__an__-no par-__lat__-o*	
Past: imperfect		**parlavo** *par-__la__-vo*	we were speaking about it yesterday
		parlavi *par-__la__-vee*	ne **parlavamo** ieri
		parlava *par-__la__-va*	*nay par-lav-__a__-mo __yer__-ee*
		parlavamo *par-lav-__a__-mo*	
		parlavate *par-lav-__a__-tay*	
		parlavano *par-__lav__-an-o*	
Future		**parlerò** *par-ler-__o__*	I'll speak to her this evening
		parlerai *par-ler-__a__-ee*	**parlerò** con lei stasera
		parlerà *par-ler-__a__*	*par-ler-__o__ kon lay sta-__ser__-a*
		parleremo *par-ler-__em__-o*	
		parlerete *par-ler-__et__-ay*	
		parleranno *par-ler-__an__-no*	
Conditional		**parlerei** *par-ler-__ay__-ee*	would you speak to him?
		parleresti *par-ler-__est__-ee*	**parleresti** con lui?
		parlerebbe *par-ler-__eb__-bay*	*par-ler-__est__-ee kon __loo__-ee?*
		parleremmo *par-ler-__em__-mo*	
		parlereste *par-ler-__est__-ay*	
		parlerebbero *par-ler-__eb__-ber-o*	
Subjunctive		**parli** *__par__-lee*	let's talk!
		parli *__par__-lee*	**parliamo!**
		parli *__par__-lee*	*parl-__ya__-mo!*
		parliamo *parl-__ya__-mo*	
		parliate *parl-__ya__-tay*	
		parlino *parl-__een__-o*	

credere (-ere verb, to believe)

Present	io	**credo** ***kred***-*o*	I don't believe it non ci **credo** *non tchee* ***kred***-*o*
	tu	**credi** ***kred***-*ee*	
	lui/lei	**crede** ***kred***-*day*	
	noi	**crediamo** *kred*-***ya***-*mo*	
	voi	**credete** *kred*-***et***-*ay*	
	loro	**credono** ***kred***-*on-o*	
Past: perfect		**ho creduto** *o kred*-***oot***-*o*	she didn't believe me non mi **ha creduto** *non mee a kred*-***oot***-*o*
		hai creduto ***a***-*ee kred*-***oot***-*o*	
		ha creduto *a kred*-***oot***-*o*	
		abbiamo creduto *ab*-***ya***-*mo kred*-***oot***-*o*	
		avete creduto *a*-***vet***-*ay kred*-***oot***-*o*	
		hanno creduto ***an***-*no kred*-***oot***-*o*	
Past: imperfect		**credevo** *kred*-***ev***-*o*	once, everyone believed in God una volta tutti **credevano** in Dio ***oo***-*na* ***vol***-*ta* ***toot***-*tee kred*-***ev***-*an-o een* ***dee***-*o*
		credevi *kred*-***ev***-*o*	
		credeva *kred*-***ev***-*a*	
		credevamo *kred*-***ev***-***a***-*mo*	
		credevate *kred-ev*-***a***-*tay*	
		credevano *kred*-***ev***-*a-no*	
Future		**crederò** *kred-er*-***o***	you'll believe me one day **mi crederai** un giorno *mee kred-er*-***a***-*ee oon* ***djorn***-*o*
		crederai *kred-er*-***a***-*ee*	
		crederà *kred-er*-***a***	
		crederemo *kred-er*-***em***-*o*	
		crederete *kred-er*-***et***-*ay*	
		crederanno *kred-er*-***an***-*no*	
Conditional		**crederei** *kred-er*-***ay***	would the police believe her? la polizia la **crederebbe**? *la pol-eets*-***ee***-*a la kred-er*-***eb***-*bay?*
		crederesti *kred-er*-***es***-*tee*	
		crederebbe *kred-er*-***eb***-*bay*	
		crederemmo *kred-er*-***em***-*mo*	
		credereste *kred-er*-***es***-*tay*	
		crederebbero *kred-er*-***eb***-*bero*	
Subjunctive		**creda** ***kred***-*a*	let's believe! **crediamo!** *kred*-***ya***-*mo!*
		creda ***kred***-*a*	
		creda ***kred***-*a*	
		crediamo *kred*-***ya***-*mo*	
		crediate *kred*-***ya***-*tay*	
		credano ***kred***-*dan-o*	

dormire (-ire verb, to sleep)

Present

io	**dormo**	***dor**-mo*
tu	**dormi**	***dor**-mee*
lui/lei	**dorme**	***dor**-may*
noi	**dormiamo**	*dorm-**ya**-mo*
voi	**dormite**	*dor-**mee**-tay*
loro	**dormono**	***dor**-mon-o*

the children are sleeping
i bambini **dormono**
*ee bam-**bee**-nee **dor**-mon-o*

Past: perfect

ho dormito *o dor-**meet**-o*
hai dormito ***a**-ee dor-**meet**-o*
ha dormito *a dor-**meet**-o*
abbiamo dormito *ab-**ya**-mo dor-**meet**-o*
avete dormito *a-**vet**-ay dor-**meet**-o*
hanno dormito ***an**-no dor-**meet**-o*

did you sleep well?
hai dormito bene?
***a**-ee dor-**meet**-o **ben**-ay?*

Past: imperfect

dormivo *dor-**mee**-vo*
dormivi *dor-**mee**-vee*
dormiva *dor-**mee**-va*
dormivamo *dor-mee-**va**-mo*
dormivate *dor-mee-**va**-tay*
dormivano *dor-**mee**-van-o*

I was sleeping when he phoned
quando ha telefonato **dormivo**
***kwand**-o a te-le-fo-**nat**-o dor-**mee**-vo*

Future

dormirò *dor-mee-**ro***
dormirai *dor-mee-**ra**-ee*
dormirà *dor-mee-**ra***
dormiremo *dor-mee-**rem**-o*
dormirete *dor-mee-**ret**-ay*
dormiranno *dor-mee-**ran**-o*

where will they sleep?
dove **dormiranno**?
***do**-vay dor-mee-**ran**-no?*

Conditional

dormirei *dor-mee-**ray**-ee*
dormiresti *dor-mee-**res**-tee*
dormirebbe *dor-mee-**reb**-bay*
dormiremmo *dor-mee-**rem**-mo*
dormireste *dor-mee-**res**-tay*
dormirebbero *dor-mee-**reb**-ber-o*

I wouldn't sleep
non **dormirei**
*non dor-mee-**ray**-ee*

Subjunctive

dorma ***dor**-ma*
dorma ***dor**-ma*
dorma ***dor**-ma*
dormiamo *dorm-**ya**-mo*
dormiate *dorm-**ya**-tay*
dormano ***dor**-man-o*

I don't think they're sleeping
non credo che **dormano**
*non **kred**-o kay **dor**-mano*

essere (to be)

Present

io	**sono** *so-no*	she's English
tu	**sei** *say*	**è** inglese
lui/lei	**è** *ay*	*e een-**glez**-ay*
noi	**siamo** *see-**a**-mo*	
voi	**siete** *see-**et**-ay*	
loro	**sono** ***so**-no*	

Past: perfect

sono stato(a) *so-no **stat**-o(a)*	I've been in London
sei stato(a) *say **stat**-o(a)*	**sono stata** a Londra
è stato(a) *ay **stat**-o(a)*	***so**-no **sta**-ta a **lon**-dra*
siamo stati(e) *see-**a**-mo **stat**-ee(ay)*	
siete stati(e) *see-**et**-tay **stat**-ee(ay)*	
sono stati(e) ***so**-no **stat**-ee(ay)*	

Past: imperfect

ero ***er**-o*	the film was very good
eri ***er**-ee*	il film **era** molto bello
era ***er**-a*	*eel feelm **er**-a **molt**-o **bel**-lo*
eravamo ***er**-a-**va**-mo*	
eravate ***er**-a-**va**-tay*	
erano ***er**-ran-o*	

Future

sarò *sa-**ro***	there'll be lots of us at the party
sarai *sa-**ra**-ee*	**saremo** in tanti alla festa
sarà *sa-**ra***	*sa-**rem**-o een **tan**-tee **al**-la **fes**-ta*
saremo *sa-**rem**-o*	
sarete *sa-**ret**-ay*	
saranno *sa-**ran**-no*	

Conditional

sarei *sa-**ray**-ee*	it would be very nice
saresti *sa-**res**-tee*	**sarebbe** molto bello
sarebbe *sa-**reb**-bay*	*sa-**reb**-bay **molt**-o **bel**-lo*
saremmo *sar-**em**-mo*	
sareste *sa-**res**-tay*	
sarebbero *sa-**reb**-ber-o*	

Subjunctive

sia ***see**-a*	I don't think it's true
sia ***see**-a*	non credo che **sia** vero
sia ***see**-a*	*non **kred**-o kay **see**-a **ver**-o*
siamo ***syam**-o*	
siate ***syat**-ay*	
siano ***syan**-o*	

stare (to be)

Present	io	**sto** *sto*	how are you?
	tu	**stai** ***sta**-ee*	come **stai**?
	lui/lei	**sta** *sta*	***kom**-ay **sta**-ee?*
	noi	**stiamo** ***styam**-o*	
	voi	**state** ***sta**-tay*	
	loro	**stanno** ***stan**-no*	
Past: perfect		**sono stato(a)** ***so**-no **stat**-o(a)*	have you ever been to Florence?
		sei stato(a) ***say**-ee **stat**-o(a)*	sei mai **stato** a Firenze?
		è stato(a) *ay **stat**-o(a)*	***say**-ee **ma**-ee **stat**-o a fee-**ren**-tsay?*
		siamo stati(e) ***syam**-o **stat**-ee(ay)*	
		siete stati(e) ***stey**-ay **stat**-ee(ay)*	
		sono stati(e) ***so**-no **stat**-ee(ay)*	
Past: imperfect		**stavo** ***sta**-vo*	it was raining
		stavi ***sta**-vee*	**stava** piovendo
		stava ***sta**-va*	***sta**-va pyo-**vend**-o*
		stavamo *sta-**va**-mo*	
		stavate *sta-**va**-tay*	
		stavano ***sta**-van-o*	
Future		**starò** *sta-**ro***	we'll be very careful
		starai *sta-**ra**-ee*	**staremo** molto attenti
		starà *sta-**ra***	*sta-**rem**-o **molt**-o at-**ten**-tee*
		staremo *sta-**rem**-o*	
		starete *sta-**ret**-ay*	
		staranno *sta-**ran**-no*	
Conditional		**starei** *sta-**ray**-ee*	she'd be better off without him
		staresti *sta-**res**-tee*	**starebbe** meglio senza di lui
		starebbe *sta-**reb**-bay*	*sta-**reb**-bay **mel**-yo **sent**-sa dee **loo**-ee*
		staremmo *sta-**rem**-mo*	
		stareste *sta-**res**-tay*	
		starebbero *sta-**reb**-ber-o*	
Subjunctive		**stia** ***stee**-a*	be careful!
		stia ***stee**-a*	**stia** attento!
		stia ***stee**-a*	***stee**-a at-**tent**-o!*
		stiamo ***styam**-o*	
		stiate ***styat**-ay*	
		stiano ***stee**-an-o*	

avere (to have)

Present

io	**ho**	*o*
tu	**hai**	***a**-ee*
lui/lei	**ha**	*a*
noi	**abbiamo**	*ab-**ya**-mo*
voi	**avete**	*a-**vet**-ay*
loro	**hanno**	***an**-no*

he has a brother and a sister
ha un fratello e una sorella
*a oon fra-**tel**-lo e **oo**-na so-**rel**-la*

Past: perfect

ho avuto *o av-**oot**-o*
hai avuto ***a**-ee av-**oot**-o*
ha avuto *a av-**oot**-o*
abbiamo avuto *ab-**ya**-mo av-**oot**-o*
avete avuto *a-**vet**-ay av-**oot**-o*
hanno avuto ***an**-no av-**oot**-o*

I had a surprise
ho avuto una sorpresa
*o av-**oot**-o **oo**-na sor-**prez**-a*

Past: imperfect

avevo *a-**vev**-o*
avevi *a-**vev**-ee*
aveva *a-**vev**-a*
avevamo *a-vev-**a**-mo*
avevate *a-vev-**a**-tay*
avevano *a-**vev**-an-o*

I had a temperature
avevo la febbre
*a-**vev**-o la **feb**-bray*

Future

avrò *av-**ro***
avrai *av-**ra**-ee*
avrà *av-**ra***
avremo *av-**rem**-o*
avrete *av-**ret**-ay*
avranno *av-**ran**-no*

they'll have more time tomorrow
domani **avranno** più tempo
***dom**-a-nee av-**ran**-no pyoo **tem**-po*

Conditional

avrei *av-**ray**-ee*
avresti *av-**res**-tee*
avrebbe *av-**reb**-bay*
avremmo *av-**rem**-mo*
avreste *av-**res**-tay*
avrebbero *av-**reb**-ber-o*

would you have ten euros?
avresti dieci euro?
*av-**res**-tee dee-**ay**-tchee **ay**-oo-ro?*

Subjunctive

abbia ***ab**-ya*
abbia ***ab**-ya*
abbia ***ab**-ya*
abbiamo *ab-**ya**-mo*
abbiate *ab-**ya**-tay*
abbiano ***ab**-ya-no*

I don't think Lidia's got flu
non credo che Lidia **abbia** l'influenza
*non **kred**-o kay **leed**-ya **ab**-ya leen-floo-**ent**-sa*

andare (to go)

Present	io	**vado** *__vad__-o*	Go away!
	tu	**vai** *__va__-ee*	**andate** via!
	lui/lei	**va** *va*	*an-__da__-tay __vee__-a!*
	noi	**andiamo** *and-__ya__-mo*	
	voi	**andate** *an-__da__-tay*	
	loro	**vanno** *__van__-no*	
Past: perfect		**sono andato(a)** *__so__-no an-__dat__-o-(a)*	how did it go?
		sei andato(a) *__say__-ee an-__dat__-o-(a)*	com'**è andata**?
		è andato(a) *e an-__dat__-o-(a)*	*__ko__-may an-__da__-ta?*
		siamo andati(e) *__syam__-o an-__dat__-ee-(ay)*	
		siete andati(e) *__syet__-ay an-__dat__-ee-(ay)*	
		sono andati(e) *__so__-no an-__dat__-ee-(ay)*	
Past: imperfect		**andavo** *an-__da__-vo*	years ago I went there a lot
		andavi *an-__da__-vee*	anni fa ci **andavo** spesso
		andava *an-__da__-va*	*__an__-nee fa tchee an-__da__-vo __spes__-so*
		andavamo *an-da-__va__-mo*	
		andavate *an-da-__va__-tay*	
		andavano *an-__da__-van-o*	
Future		**andrò** *and-__ro__*	where will you go?
		andrai *and-__ra__-ee*	dove **andrai**?
		andrà *and-__ra__*	*__dov__-ay and-__ra__-ee?*
		andremo *and-__rem__-o*	
		andrete *and-__ret__-ay*	
		andranno *and-__ran__-no*	
Conditional		**andrei** *and-__ray__-ee*	maybe it would go better
		andresti *and-__res__-tee*	forse **andrebbe** meglio
		andrebbe *and-__reb__-bay*	*__for__-say and-__reb__-bay __mel__-yo*
		andremmo *and-__rem__-mo*	
		andreste *and-__res__-tay*	
		andrebbero *and-__reb__-ber-o*	
Subjunctive		**vada** *__va__-da*	I hope it goes well
		vada *__va__-da*	spero che **vada** bene
		vada *__va__-da*	*__sper__-o kay __va__-da __ben__-ay*
		andiamo *and-__ya__-mo*	
		andiate *and-__ya__-tay*	
		vadano *__va__-da-no*	

fare (to do, to make)

Present	io	**faccio** ***fa***-*tcho*	it doesn't matter
	tu	**fai** ***fa***-*ee*	**fa** niente
	lui/lei	**fa** *fa*	*fa* ***nyen***-*tay*
	noi	**facciamo** *fatch*-***a***-*mo*	
	voi	**fate** ***fa***-*tay*	
	loro	**fanno** ***fan***-*no*	
Past: perfect		**ho fatto** *o* ***fat***-*to*	I've made the beds
		hai fatto ***a***-*ee* ***fat***-*to*	**ho fatto** i letti
		ha fatto *a* ***fat***-*to*	*o* ***fat***-*to ee* ***let***-***tee***
		abbiamo fatto *ab*-***bya***-*mo* ***fat***-*to*	
		avete fatto *a*-***vet***-*ay* ***fat***-*to*	
		hanno fatto ***an***-*no* ***fat***-*to*	
Past: imperfect		**facevo** *fa*-***tchev***-*o*	what was she doing?
		facevi *fa*-***tchev***-*ee*	cosa **faceva**?
		faceva *fa*-***tchev***-*a*	***ko***-*za fa*-***tchev***-*a?*
		facevamo *fa-tchev*-***a***-*mo*	
		facevate *fa-tchev*-***a***-*tay*	
		facevano *fa*-***tchev***-*a-no*	
Future		**farò** *fa*-***ro***	I'll do it tomorrow
		farai *fa*-***ra***-*ee*	lo **farò** domani
		farà *fa*-***ra***	*lo fa*-***ro*** *dom*-***a***-*nee*
		faremo *fa*-***rem***-*o*	
		farete *far*-***ret***-*ay*	
		faranno *fa*-***ran***-*no*	
Conditional		**farei** *fa*-***ray***-*ee*	I don't know what I'd do
		faresti *fa*-***res***-*tee*	non so che cosa **farei**
		farebbe *fa*-***reb***-*bay*	*non so kay* ***ko***-*za fa*-***ray***
		faremmo *fa*-***rem***-*mo*	
		fareste *fa*-***res***-*tay*	
		farebbero *fa*-***reb***-*ber-o*	
Subjunctive		**faccia** ***fa***-*tcha*	please do!
		faccia ***fa***-*tcha*	**faccia** pure!
		faccia *fa*-***tcha***	***fa***-*tcha* ***poo***-*ray!*
		facciamo *fatch*-***a***-*mo*	
		facciate *fa*-***tcha***-*tay*	
		facciano ***fa***-*tchan-o*	

potere (to be able)

Present	io	**posso** *__pos__-so*	can you come with us?
	tu	**puoi** *pwoy*	**puoi** venire con noi?
	lui/lei	**può** *pwo*	*pwoy ven-__ee__-ray kon noy?*
	noi	**possiamo** *poss-__ya__-mo*	
	voi	**potete** *po-__tet__-ay*	
	loro	**possono** *__pos__-son-o*	
Past: perfect		**ho potuto** *o pot-__oot__-o*	I couldn't do it yesterday
		hai potuto *__a__-ee pot-__oot__-o*	non **ho potuto** farlo ieri
		ha potuto *a pot-__oot__-o*	*non o pot-__oot__-o __far__-lo __yer__-ee*
		abbiamo potuto *ab-__ya__-mo pot-__oot__-o*	
		avete potuto *a-__vet__-ay pot-__oot__-o*	
		hanno potuto *__an__-no pot-__oot__-o*	
Past: imperfect		**potevo** *po-__tev__-o*	I couldn't do any more of it
		potevi *po-__tev__-ee*	non ne **potevo** più
		poteva *po-__tev__-a*	*non nay po-__tev__-o pyoo*
		potevamo *po-tev-__am__-o*	
		potevate *po-tev-__at__-ay*	
		potevano *po-__tev__-an-o*	
Future		**potrò** *pot-__ro__*	we won't be able to come tomorrow
		potrai *pot-__ra__-ee*	non **potremo** venire domani
		potrà *pot-__ra__*	*non pot-__rem__-o ven-__eer__-ay dom-__a__-nee*
		potremo *pot-__rem__-o*	
		potrete *pot-__ret__-ay*	
		potranno *pot-__ran__-no*	
Conditional		**potrei** *pot-__ray__-ee*	it could happen
		potresti *pot-__res__-tee*	**potrebbe** succedere
		potrebbe *pot-__reb__-bay*	*pot-__reb__-be soo-__tched__-er-ay*
		potremmo *pot-__rem__-mo*	
		potreste *pot-__res__-tay*	
		potrebbero *pot-__reb__-ber-o*	
Subjunctive		**possa** *__pos__-sa*	I hope Luigi can come
		possa *__pos__-sa*	spero che Luigi **possa** venire
		possa *__pos__-sa*	*__sper__-o kay loo-__ee__-djee __pos__-sa ven-__ee__-ray*
		possiamo *poss-__ya__-mo*	
		possiate *poss-__ya__-tay*	
		possano *__poss__-an-o*	

volere (to want)

Present	io	**voglio** ***vol***-*yo*	what do you want?
	tu	**vuoi** *vwoy*	cosa **vuoi**?
	lui/lei	**vuole** ***vwo***-*lay*	***ko***-*za vwoy?*
	noi	**vogliamo** *vol*-***ya***-*mo*	
	voi	**volete** *vo*-***let***-*ay*	
	loro	**vogliono** ***vol***-*yo-no*	
Past: perfect		**ho voluto** *o vol*-***oot***-*o*	he didn't want to admit it
		hai voluto ***a***-*ee vol*-***oot***-*o*	non **ha voluto** ammetterlo
		ha voluto *a vol*-***oot***-*o*	*non a vol*-***oot***-*o am*-***met***-*ter-lo*
		abbiamo voluto *ab*-***ya***-*mo vol*-***oot***-*o*	
		avete voluto *a*-***vet***-*ay vol*-***oot***-*o*	
		hanno voluto ***an***-*no vol*-***oot***-*o*	
Past: imperfect		**volevo** *vo*-***lev***-*o*	she wanted to dance
		volevi *vo*-***lev***-*ee*	**voleva** ballera
		voleva *vo*-***lev***-*a*	*vo*-***lev***-*a bal*-***la***-*ray*
		volevamo *vo-lev*-***a***-*mo*	
		volevate *vo-lev*-***a***-*tay*	
		volevano *vo*-***lev***-*a-no*	
Future		**vorrò** *vor*-***ro***	will you want to get married?
		vorrai *vor*-***ra***-*ee*	**vorrei** sposarti?
		vorrà *vor*-***ra***	*vor*-***ray***-*ee spoz*-***ar***-*tee?*
		vorremo *vor*-***rem***-*o*	
		vorrete *vor*-***ret***-*ay*	
		vorranno *vor*-***ran***-*no*	
Conditional		**vorrei** *vor*-***ray***-*ee*	I'd like to go to Australia
		vorresti *vor*-***res***-*tee*	**vorrei** andare in Australia
		vorrebbe *vor*-***reb***-*bay*	*vor*-***ray***-*ee an*-***da***-*ray een aoo*-***stral***-*ya*
		vorremmo *vor*-***rem***-*mo*	
		vorreste *vor*-***res***-*tay*	
		vorrebbero *vor*-***reb***-*ber-o*	
Subjunctive		**voglia** ***vol***-*ya*	I hope Luigi wants to come
		voglia ***vol***-*ya*	spero che Luigi **voglia** venire
		voglia ***vol***-*ya*	***sper***-*o kay loo*-***ee***-*djee* ***vol***-*ya ven*-***ee***-*ray*
		vogliamo *vol*-***ya***-*mo*	
		vogliate *vol*-***ya***-*tay*	
		vogliano ***vol***-*yan-o*	

dovere (to have to)

Present

io	**devo**	***dev**-o*
tu	**devi**	***dev**-ee*
lui/lei	**deve**	***dev**-ay*
noi	**dobbiamo**	*dob-**ya**-mo*
voi	**dovete**	*do-**vet**-ay*
loro	**devono**	***dev**-on-o*

it must be late
dev'essere tardi
*dev-**es**-ser-ay **tar**-dee*

Past: perfect

ho dovuto *o dov-**oot**-o*
hai dovuto ***a**-ee dov-**oot**-o*
ha dovuto *a dov-**oot**-o*
abbiamo dovuto *ab-**ya**-mo dov-**oot**-o*
avete dovuto *a-**vet**-ay dov-**oot**-o*
hanno dovuto ***an**-no dov-**oot**-o*

I had to tell him
ho dovuto dirglielo
*o dov-**oot**-o **deerl**-yel-o*

Past: imperfect

dovevo *do-**vev**-o*
dovevi *do-**vev**-ee*
doveva *do-**vev**-a*
dovevamo *do-vev-**a**-mo*
dovevate *do-vev-**a**-tay*
dovevano *do-**vev**-an-o*

you shouldn't have!
non **dovevi!**
*non do-**vev**-ee!*

Future

dovrò *dov-**ro***
dovrai *dov-**ra**-ee*
dovrà *dov-**ra***
dovremo *dov-**rem**-o*
dovrete *dov-**ret**-ay*
dovranno *dov-**ran**-no*

we'll have to do it again
dovremo rifarlo
*dov-**rem**-o ree-**far**-lo*

Conditional

dovrei *dov-**ray**-ee*
dovresti *dov-**res**-tee*
dovrebbe *dov-**reb**-bay*
dovremmo *dov-**rem**-mo*
dovreste *dov-**res**-tay*
dovrebbero *dov-**reb**-ber-o*

you should help him
dovresti aiutarlo
*dov-**res**-tee a-yoo-**tar**-lo*

Subjunctive

deva ***dev**-a*
deva ***dev**-a*
deva ***dev**-a*
dobbiamo *dob-**ya**-mo*
dobbiate *dob-**ya**-tay*
devano ***dev**-an-o*

I think they have to go
credo che **devano** partire
***kred**-o kay **dev**-ano par-**tee**-ray*

dare (to give)

Present	io	**do** *doh*	Aunt Maria gives us sweets Zia Maria ci **dà** le caramelle ***dze**-a ma-**ree**-a tchee da lay ka-ra-**mel**-lay*
	tu	**dai** ***da**-ee*	
	lui/lei	**dà** *da*	
	noi	**diamo** ***dyam**-o*	
	voi	**date** ***da**-tay*	
	loro	**danno** ***dan**-no*	
Past: perfect		**ho dato** *o **dat**-o*	He gave me a book Mi **ha dato** un libro *mee a **dat**-o oon **leeb**-ro*
		hai dato ***a**-ee **dat**-o*	
		ha dato *a **dat**-o*	
		abbiamo dato *ab-**ya**-mo **dat**-o*	
		avete dato *a-**vet**-ay **dat**-o*	
		hanno dato ***an**-no **dat**-o*	
Past: imperfect		**davo** ***da**-vo*	they gave me my salary every month mi **davano** lo stipendio ogni mese *mee **da**-van-o lo stee-**pend**-yo **on**-yee **mez**-ay*
		davi ***da**-vee*	
		dava ***da**-va*	
		davamo *da-**va**-mo*	
		davate *da-**va**-tay*	
		davano ***da**-van-o*	
Future		**darò** *da-**ro***	They'll give me an answer tomorrow mi **daranno** una risposta domani *mee da-**ran**-no **oo**-na rees-**pos**-ta dom-**a**-nee*
		darai *da-**ra**-ee*	
		darà *da-**ra***	
		daremo *da-**rem**-o*	
		darete *da-**ret**-ay*	
		daranno *da-**ran**-no*	
Conditional		**darei** *da-**ray**-ee*	would you take a look? **daresti** un'occhiata? *da-**res**-tee oon-ok-**kya**-ta?*
		daresti *da-**res**-tee*	
		darebbe *da-**reb**-bay*	
		daremmo *da-**rem**-mo*	
		dareste *da-**res**-tay*	
		darebbero *da-**reb**-ber-o*	
Subjunctive		**dia** ***dee**-a*	give me a kilo mi **dia** un chilo *mee **dee**-a oon **kee**-lo*
		dia ***dee**-a*	
		dia ***dee**-a*	
		diamo ***dyam**-o*	
		diate ***dyat**-ay*	
		diano ***dyan**-o*	

lavarsi (to wash oneself)

Present

io	**mi lavo** *mee **la**-vo*	he's washing in the lake
tu	**ti lavi** *tee **la**-vee*	**si lava** nel lago
lui/lei	**si lava** *see **la**-va*	*see **la**-va nel **la**-go*
noi	**ci laviamo** *tchee lav-**ya**-mo*	
voi	**vi lavate** *vee lav-**a**-tay*	
loro	**si lavano** *see **lav**-an-o*	

Past: perfect

mi sono lavato(a) *mee **so**-no la-**vat**-o(a)*
ti sei lavato(a) *tee **say**-ee la-**vat**-o(a)*
si è lavato(a) *see ay la-**vat**-o(a)*
ci siamo lavati(e) *tchee **syam**-o la-**va**-tee(ay)*
vi siete lavati(e) *vee **syet**-ay (la-**va**-tee(ay)*
si sono lavati(e) *see **so**-no la-**va**-tee(ay)*

did you wash your hands?
ti **sei lavato** le mani?
*tee **say**-ee la-**vat**-o lay **ma**-nee?*

Past: imperfect

mi lavavo *mee la-**va**-vo*
ti lavavi *tee la-**va**-vee*
si lavava *see la-**va**-va*
ci lavavamo *tchee la-va-**va**-mo*
vi lavavate *vee la-va-**va**-tay*
si lavavano *see la-**va**-van-o*

years ago we used to wash in front of the fire
anni fa **ci lavavamo** davanti al fuoco
***an**-nee fa tchee la-va-**va**-mo da-**van**-tee al **fwo**-ko*

Future

mi laverò *mee la-ver-**o***
ti laverai *tee la-ver-**a**-ee*
si laverà *see la-ver-**a***
ci laveremo *chee la-ver-**em**-o*
vi laverete *vee la-ver-**et**-ay*
si laveranno *see la-ver-**an**-no*

I'll wash in the bathroom
mi laverò in bagno
*mee la-ver-**o** een **ban**-yo*

Conditional

mi laverei *mee la-ver-**ay**-ee*
ti laveresti *tee la-ver-**es**-tee*
si laverebbe *see la-ver-**eb**-bay*
ci laveremmo *tchee la-ver-**em**-mo*
vi lavereste *vee la-ver-**es**-tay*
si laverebbero *see la-ver-**eb**-ber-o*

would you wash in this place?
ti laveresti in questo posto?
*tee la-ver-**es**-tee een **kwes**-to **post**-o?*

Subjunctive

mi lavi *mee **la**-vee*
ti lavi *tee **la**-vee*
si lavi *see **la**-vee*
ci laviamo *tchee lav-**ya**-mo*
vi laviate *vee lav-**ya**-tay*
si lavino *see lav-**een**-o*

let's wash straight away!
laviamoci subito!
*lav-**ya**-mo-tchee **soo**-beet-o!*